Cats & Kittens
in Acrylics

Julie Nash

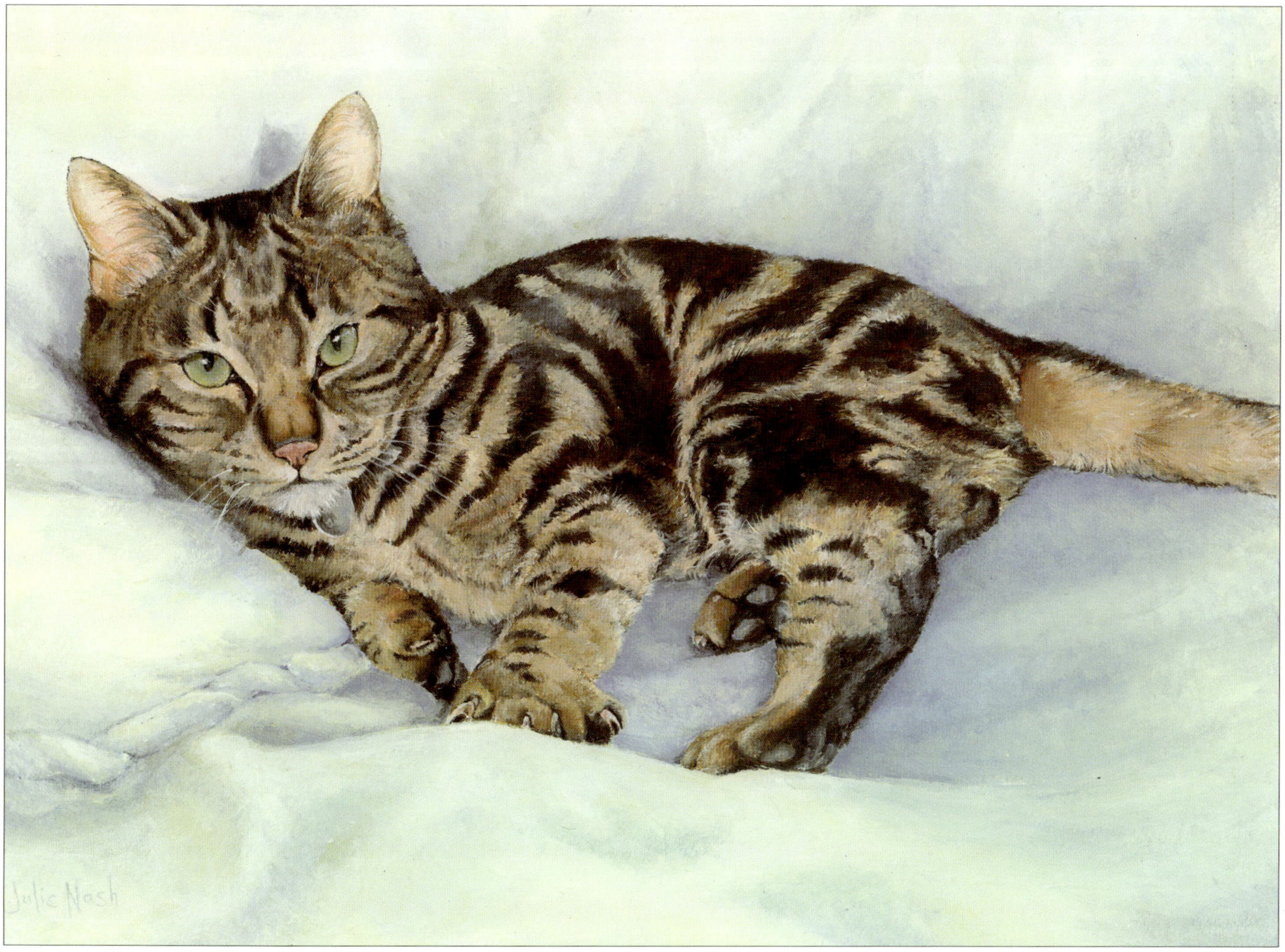

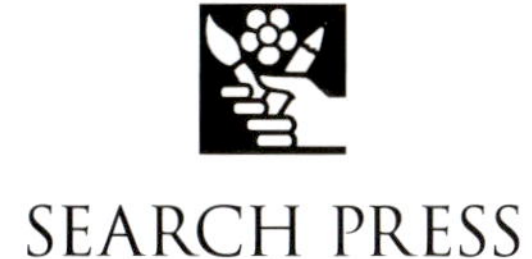

SEARCH PRESS

First published in Great Britain 2012

Search Press Limited
Wellwood, North Farm Road,
Tunbridge Wells, Kent TN2 3DR

Text copyright © Julie Nash, 2012

Photographs by Paul Bricknell at Search Press Studios

Photographs and design copyright © Search Press Ltd, 2012

ISBN: 978-1-84448-716-5

Suppliers
If you have any difficulty obtaining any of the materials and equipment mentioned in this book, please visit the Search Press website:
www.searchpress.com

Publishers' notes
All the step-by-step photographs in this book feature the author, Julie Nash, demonstrating her acrylic painting techniques. No models have been used.

Please note: when removing the perforated sheets of tracing paper from the book, score them first, then carefully pull out each sheet.

Share your Ready to Paint artworks with the world. Simply go to the 'Ready to Paint' page on Facebook and upload your images.

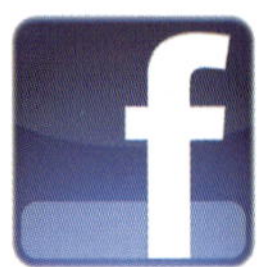

Printed in China

Dedication

I dedicate this book to my mum, Jean Moran. Her quiet support for me, her last 'little chick', is without limit.

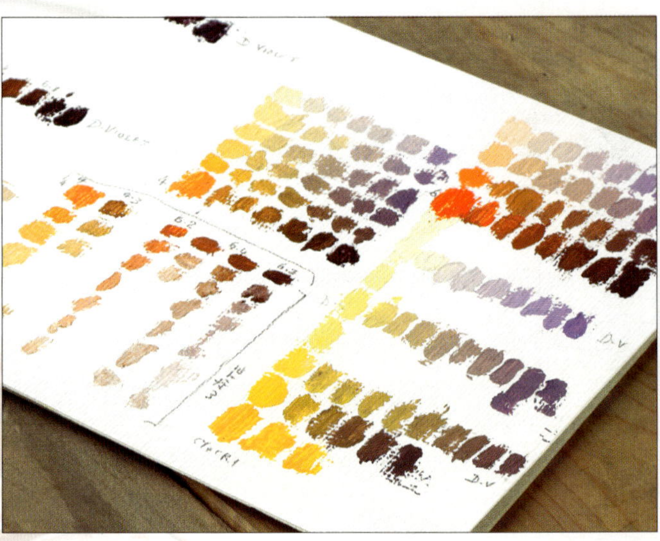

Acknowledgements

I would like to thank my editor, Alison Shaw, and photographer, Paul Bricknell. It was a joy to work with you both. Also, Roz Dace, Juan Hayward and all the creative people at Search Press, who make it all happen. Special thanks must be made to Lisa McLinden and Phil Harrison who generously allowed me into their homes to meet their cats. It was a pleasure and an honour. My students also deserve a mention; they brighten my days and it is a privilege to be their teacher.

Page 1
Purrfect Comfort
42 x 30cm (16½ x 11¾in)

Cats seem to be born with the instinct for finding the most comfortable places and claiming them as their own. This one is no exception, having claimed his favourite spot on the bed. Am I the only person to make the bed around the cats so I don't disturb their slumbers?

Opposite
Paws for Thought
42 x 30cm (16½ x 11¾in)

Have you ever wondered what cats are thinking about when they stare off into space? Having settled on a sunny bit of carpet, this one looks wide awake but is miles away as it soaks up the warmth.

Contents

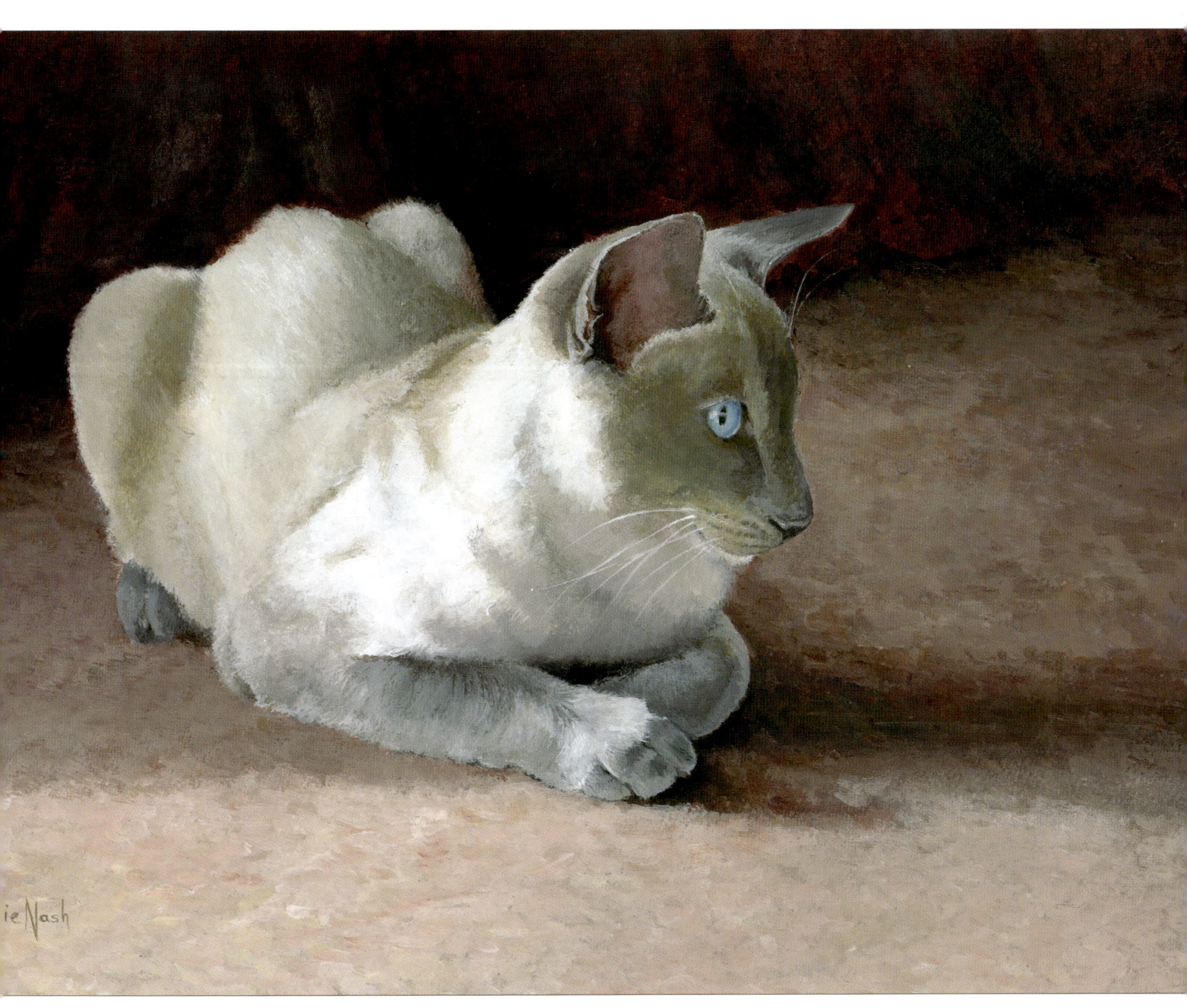

Introduction

Animals are one of my favourite subjects to paint and were probably the first things I tried to do as a child. There is enormous satisfaction in achieving a likeness, whether it is by catching the expression in the eyes, the coat of soft fur or a natural pose.

Seeing and feeling how paint moves and mixes when you work is exciting too. Each time you paint a picture, you learn something new about colours and what your paints and brushes can do for you. I believe art should be enjoyable and relaxing. I also think it is good for it to be just a little bit challenging too. This is because, if we can stretch ourselves a little, we gain the most satisfaction and learn something that will make us better artists next time we paint.

However, we all need a little help along the way and it is better to focus our efforts on specific skills and tackle things in small steps. This is where the tracings really help. By using the tracings and following the step-by-step demonstrations, you don't have to worry about the drawing, leaving you free to concentrate on enjoying painting each of these lovely felines. Take a look at page 9 to see how I transfer the tracings to my paper. It is so easy and you can use the tracings many times over. By looking at and using the tracings, I hope you will also gain an insight into how I reduce all the complicated visual information into a working drawing. This will help you get a feel for drawing so that when you are ready to 'go it alone' with your own drawings, you will already have an intuitive feel for how it is done.

I want you to enjoy each step, gain confidence, and feel excited about trying the next project, so I have arranged the demonstrations so that you can enjoy discovering your talents at a comfortable pace. You can try these paintings again and again, repeating each one as often as you need to. You don't have to stick to my colour schemes either. As you become more confident, you can try making your own changes and here and there I have made a few suggestions to get you started. When you feel ready to have a go at a painting without a step-by-step demonstration, you can try the one shown here, using the bonus tracing, number 6.

Happy painting!

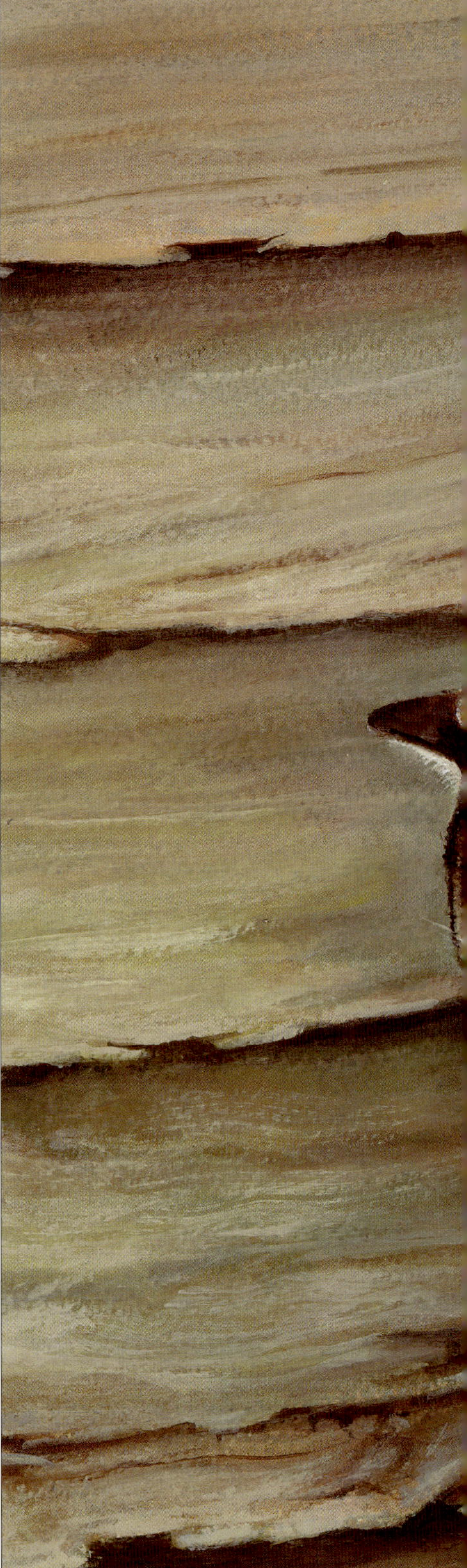

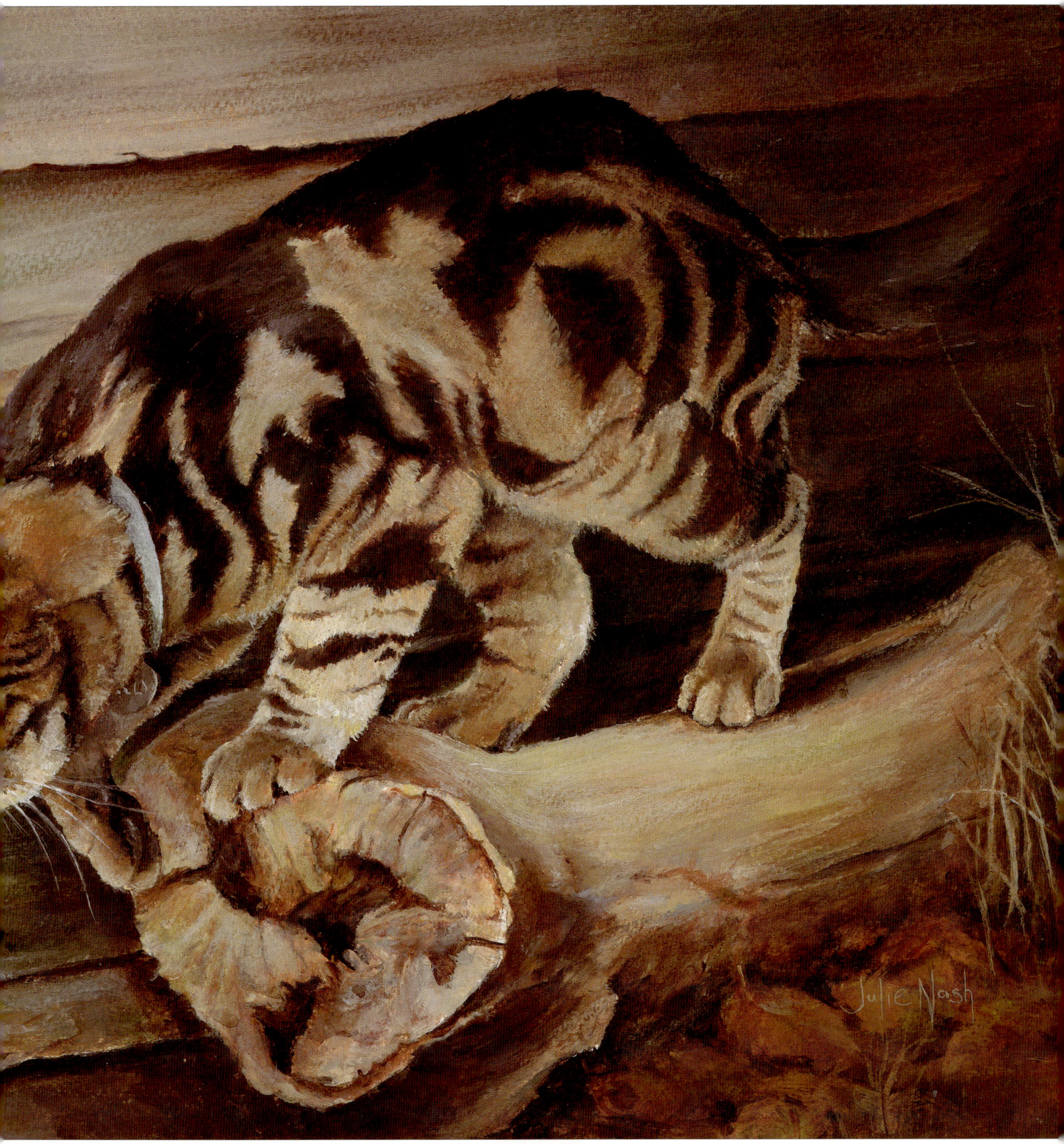

TRACING

6

Woodland Explorer

42 x 30cm (16½ x 11¾in)

Inside every cat and kitten is an intrepid explorer. This little adventurer is emerging into the sunlight, from the depth of the 'wild wood' at the end of the garden.

Materials

Paints

Acrylic paint is a very versatile medium. I love the way it can be used thinly in washes and the buttery feel it has when used undiluted. Once dry, the paint film is impervious to water. This means that you can easily paint over an area, to change the colour or make subtle effects without muddying the colours. Watch out though, if it dries on your clothes it won't wash out. You can use acrylics on paper, canvas, wood and even metal with a suitable primer.

I use artists' quality paints as these give the best results and are reliable, high-quality products. With their higher ratio of pigment, a little paint goes a long way so you get plenty for your money.

My basic palette is titanium white, cadmium yellow, lemon yellow, cadmium red, alizarin crimson, French ultramarine, cobalt blue, Prussian blue, yellow ochre, raw sienna, burnt sienna, burnt umber, raw umber, Hooker's green and deep violet. I don't buy black paint as I prefer to mix my own darks as these sit more comfortably in a painting and have greater depth and richness compared to commercially available black.

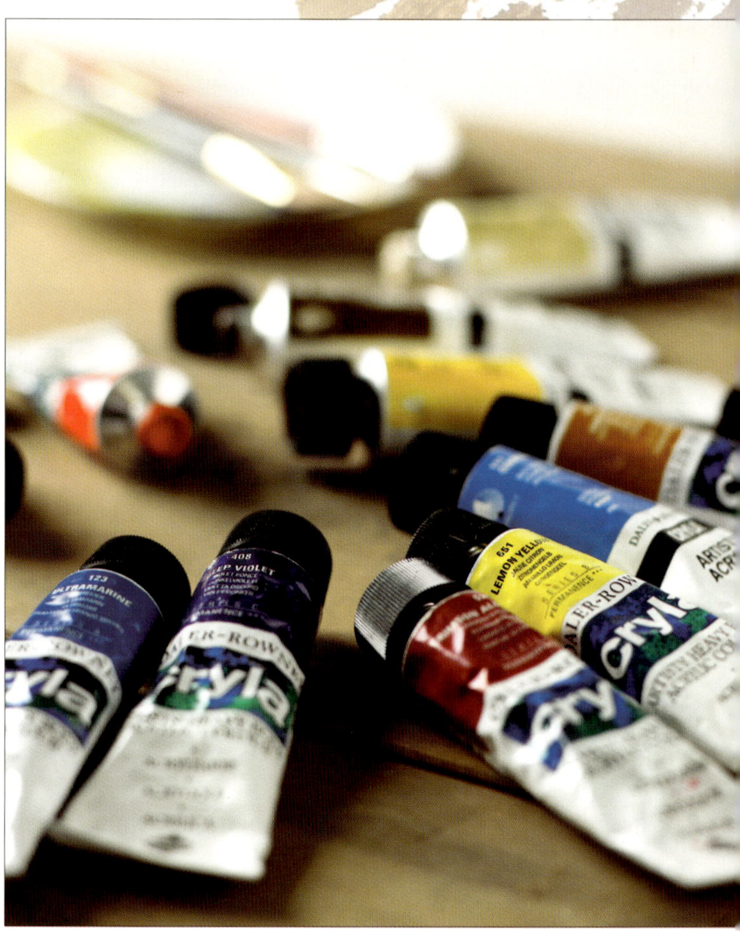

A selection of acrylic paints in tubes.

300gsm (140lb) Not paper, suitable for all the projects in this book.

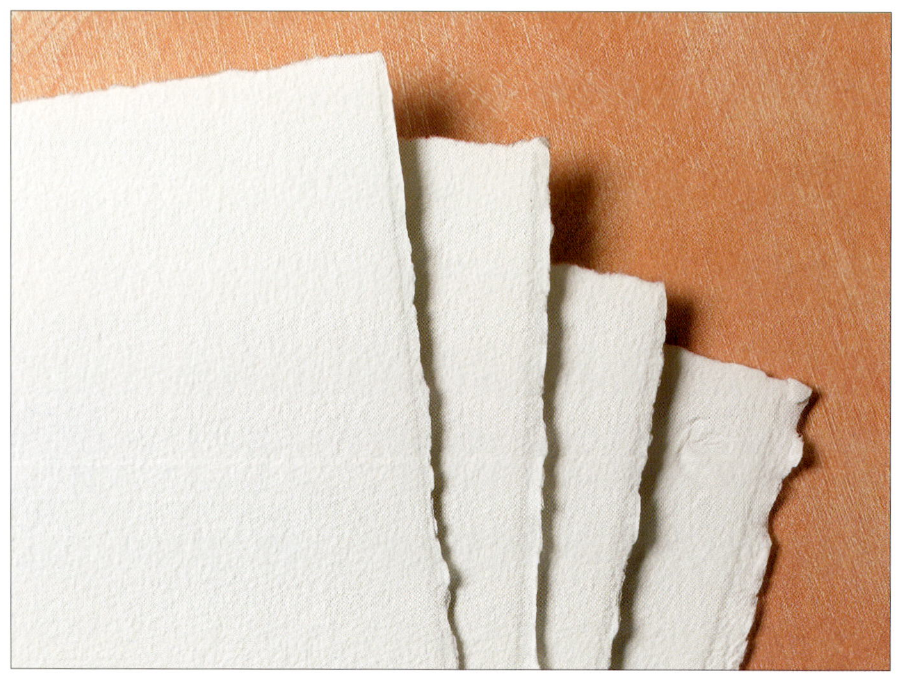

Paper

When working on paper I use a 300gsm (140lb) or heavier watercolour paper, in either a Rough or Not (cold-pressed) finish. Both of these have a nice surface texture that will allow you to use scumbling and dry brush techniques. Rough has the most surface texture so will give a more broken effect. Hot-pressed (HP) paper is very smooth, like cartridge paper so I only use this type when I need to do very tightly detailed work.

All the paintings in this book have been painted on stretched 300gsm (140lb) Not watercolour paper.

Brushes

I prefer to use good quality synthetic brushes as they have a nice spring to the fibres and good holding capacity. Another bonus is that they can be easily cleaned with warm water and a little liquid hand soap at the end of each session. I look for brushes that form a good point (round brushes) or a chiselled edge (flat brushes). Avoid buying cheap sets of brushes, as they will probably disappoint you and hinder your progress. Instead, look for sets of quality brushes or buy a few well-chosen sizes and shapes.

For the demonstrations in this book I used the following brushes for blocking in backgrounds and painting the fur: 3mm (1/8in), 5mm (3/16in), 6mm (1/4in), 10mm (3/8in), 13mm (1/2in), 15mm (5/8in), 19mm (3/4in) flats, and filberts in sizes 2 and 6. Use the largest brushes for blocking in and gradually use smaller brushes as you work up the painting and refine the details. You will know it is time to use a smaller brush when the one you are using starts to feel too cumbersome. If, when following the demonstrations, you feel uncomfortable with the size I have used, please change to a size you do feel comfortable with. With practice you will discover that you can use larger brushes for smaller jobs as you increase your control of the brush.

I use small round brushes (size 1 or 3) to re-draw over the tracing lines with thinned colour. This fixes the drawing and makes it easier to see. I also use these for finer details like whiskers and highlights in the eyes. My other round brushes are sizes 2, 4, and 6. As brushes begin to wear, they are downgraded from best brushes and used for scrubbing in base colours or any other task that would quickly dull a good brush.

Stay-wet palette

A stay-wet palette is an essential bit of kit. Acrylic paint dries very quickly and this type of palette will keep paint moist for a long time – weeks if necessary. It consists of a shallow plastic box with a close-fitting lid. Inside this box you place a sheet of reservoir paper. Water is then added to this until it is fully saturated. On top of this, you lay a sheet of membrane paper. Your paint is placed on top of this layer. The membrane paper allows water to pass through from the reservoir paper, into the paint, replacing that lost by evaporation. When the lid is closed, the palette maintains a moist atmosphere around the paint, preventing drying so you don't have to keep mixing fresh paint each time you take a break. During painting, if you see the membrane paper starting to dry out and curl, it is a sign that the water content in the reservoir paper is getting low. Slightly peel back the membrane paper and add a little more water to the reservoir layer, before lightly pressing down the membrane sheet.

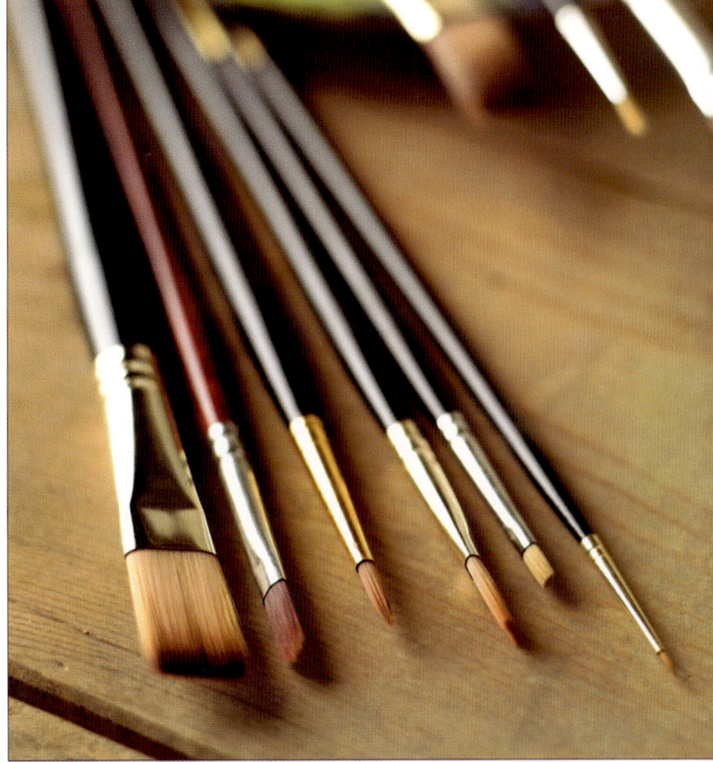

Above and below: a selection of brushes used in this book.

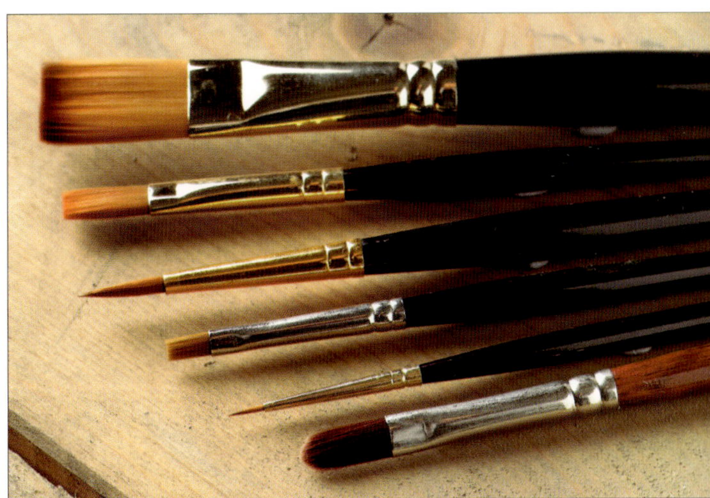

Below: my stay-wet palette.

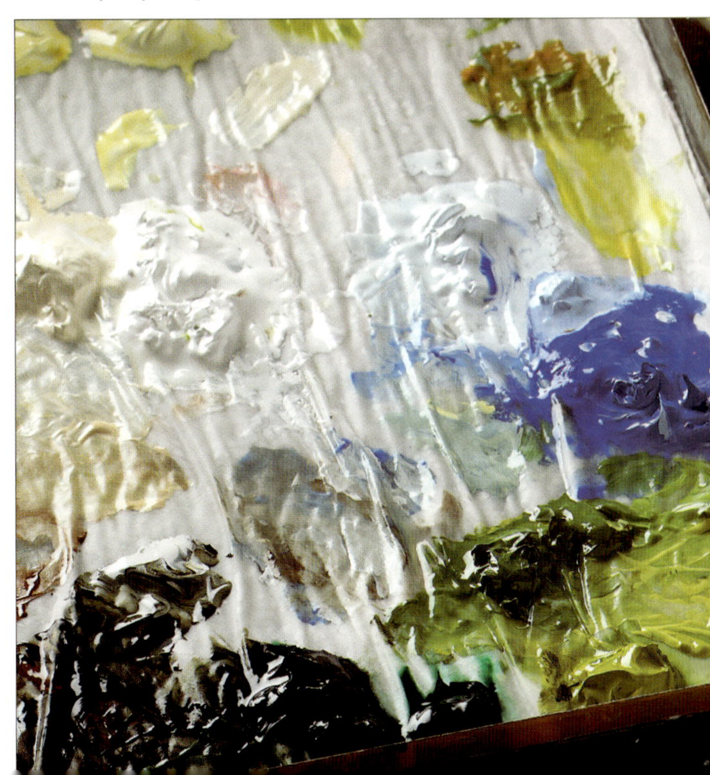

Other materials

Two short, wide glass jars I have one for rinsing out brushes and the other for moistening a fresh brush and diluting paint when I need it to flow more easily.

White ceramic side plates These are useful for mixing colours before adding them to your stay-wet palette.

A small metal-bladed palette knife This is used to mix the paint. I avoid using plastic equipment as I find that the paint sticks to plastic and is impossible to remove. Glass, metal and ceramic tools can be cleaned very easily.

Graphite paper I use a sheet of graphite paper to place under the tracings. I find this is quicker than scribbling pencil over the back and it is easier to see the original lines of the tracing. You can also reposition the tracing over the painting, at intervals, to check things are not getting out of shape.

Dried-out ballpoint pen This is used for transferring the tracing. This gives a firm point that easily transfers the graphite on to your paper.

Kitchen paper This has many uses. I place a few sheets under the water jars to mop up any spills and for wiping excess paint off the brushes before rinsing them in the water. It can also be used to wipe wet paint off the painting.

Spray bottle One with a fine misting action is useful to have when working in warm conditions. It can be used to mist over both your palette and your painting to slightly slow down the drying time.

Drawing board Made from 12mm (½in) thick plywood to hold the stretched watercolour paper. Unless you have to transport your paper during painting, avoid thinner boards as they often warp as the paper dries.

Paper gummed-tape This is used to secure wet paper to the drawing board when stretching.

Masking tape This is applied around the edge of the picture area to give a clean edge to the finished painting. It also protects the paper gummed-tape from moisture during painting.

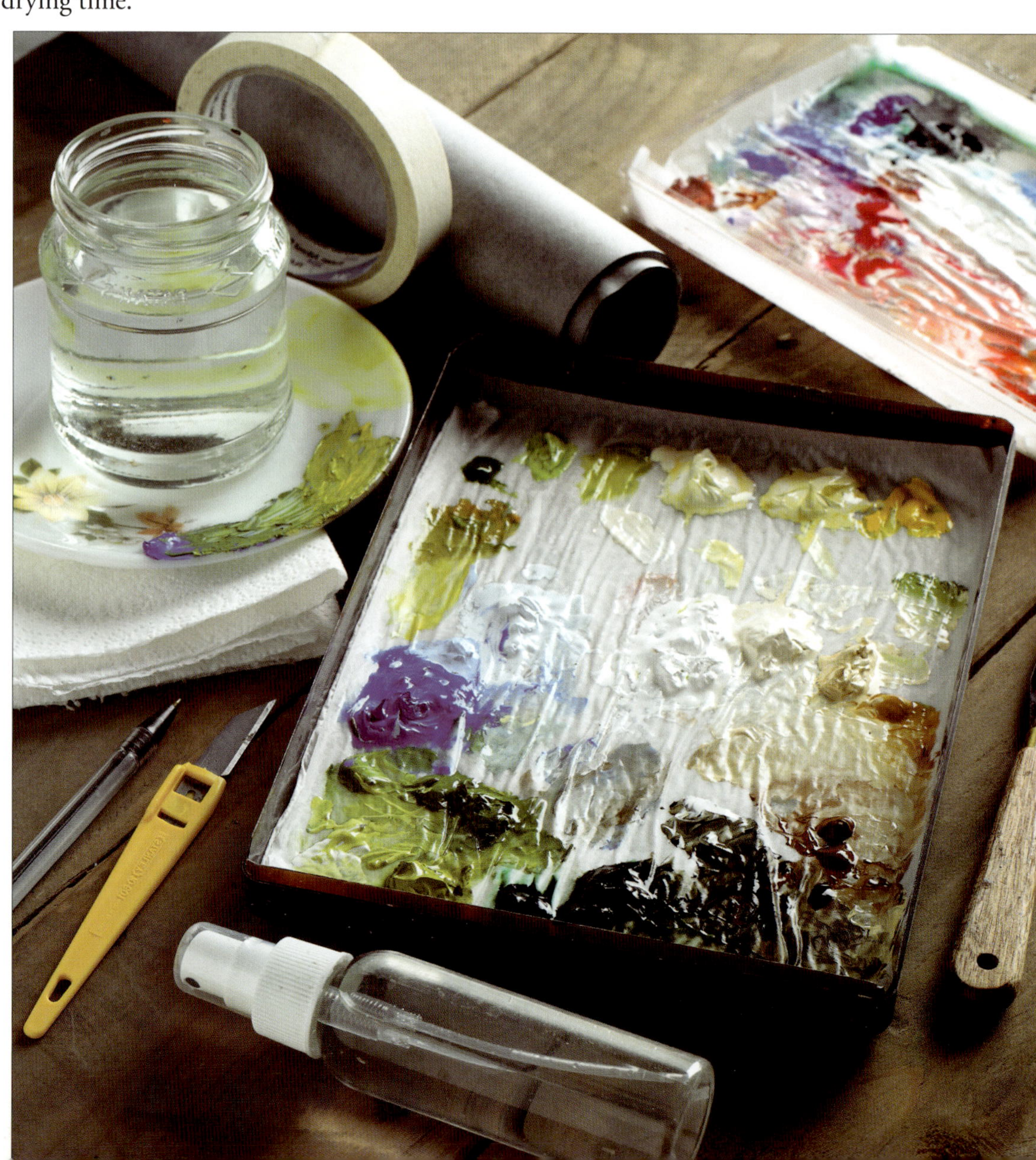

Transferring the image

This is really easy. Pull out the tracing from the front of the book and follow
the steps below. You can reuse the tracings many times. If you prefer not to use
graphite paper, you can scribble soft pencil over the back of the tracing sheet
before positioning it over the paper.

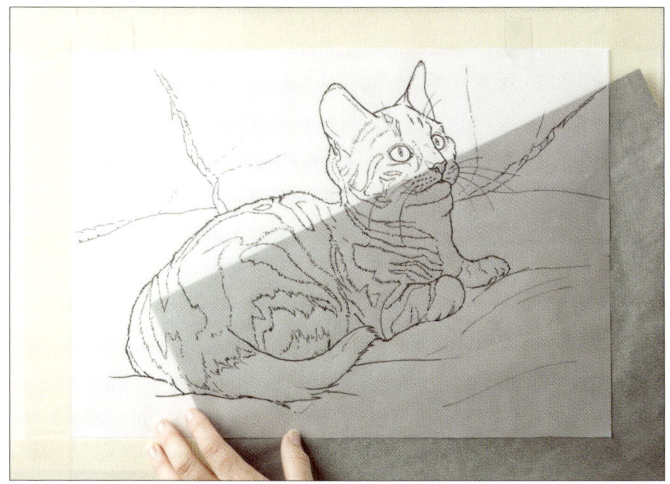

1 On dry, stretched paper, apply strips of masking
tape around the outside edges of the painting area.
Lay the tracing over your stretched paper and secure in
place with two tabs of sticky tape on the top edge. Place
a sheet of graphite paper underneath the tracing paper.

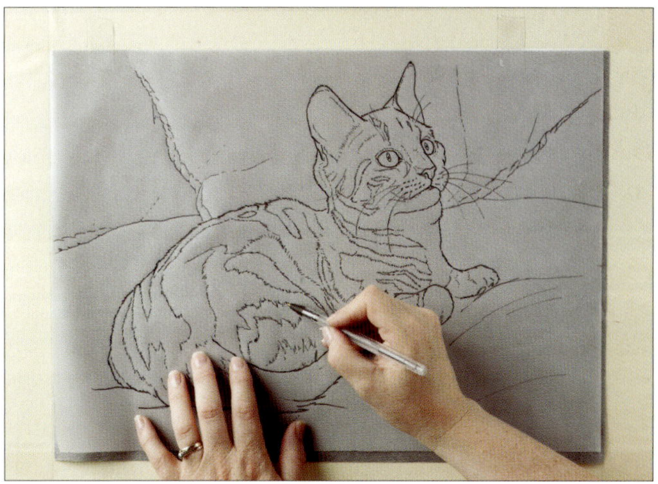

2 Using a hard, fine-pointed implement such as a
dried-out ballpoint pen, go over the lines on the tracing.
I prefer this method of tracing as I find it is easier to see
the tracing lines, compared to when pencil is scribbled
over the back of the tracing.

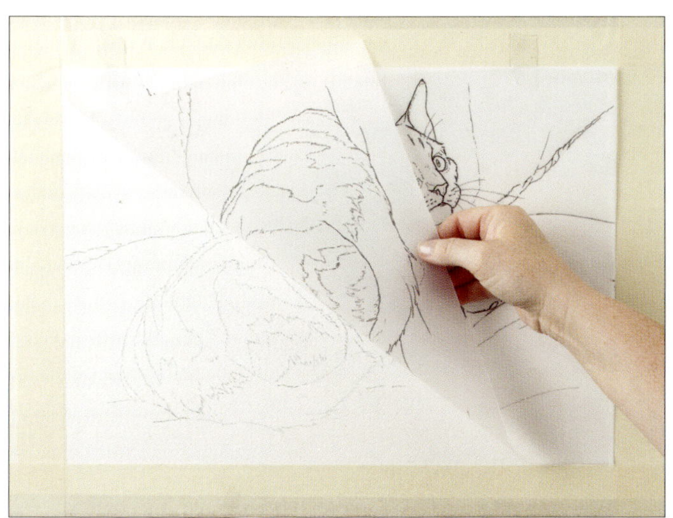

3 As you work across the tracing, lift the graphite
paper a couple of times to check that you are using just
enough pressure to leave a graphite drawing on
the paper.

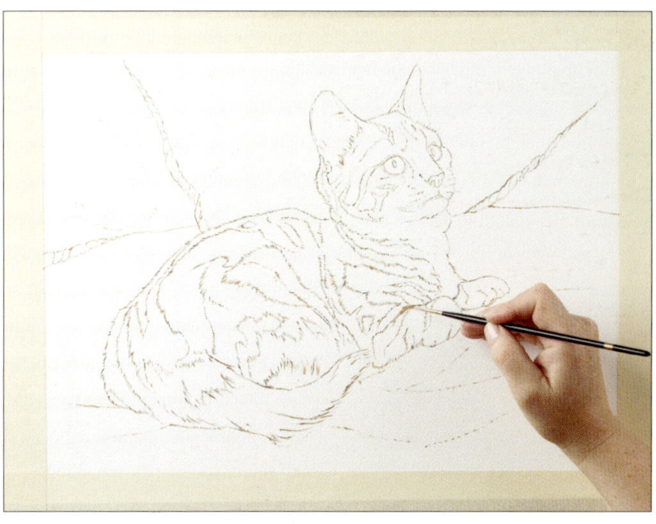

4 With the tracing complete, use a little thinned paint
and a fine brush to redraw the lines. This gives a
permanent drawing that won't smudge as soon as you
start painting and it gives you an opportunity to check
you have the complete drawing on the paper.

Ginger Delight

This little ginger tabby was settled in his favourite spot when a flock of starlings landed on the glass roof, right above us. He was a little startled, but intensely curious about these strange creatures. I think this picture captures that moment of discovery and indecision.

Tip

If the paper is dry or dragging as you paint, spray on a touch of water to moisten it.

You will need

300gsm (140lb) Rough or Not watercolour paper

Colours: raw sienna, burnt sienna, cadmium yellow, cerulean blue, titanium white, Hooker's green, French ultramarine, cadmium red, raw umber, burnt umber, deep violet, cobalt blue

Brushes: size 1 round, size 2 round, size 3 round, 3mm (⅛in) flat, 6mm (¼in) flat, 13mm (½in) flat, 15mm (⅝in) flat, size 2 filbert, size 6 filbert

Eraser

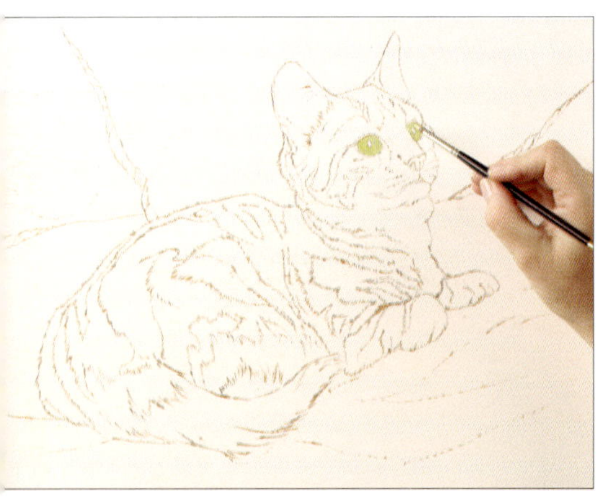

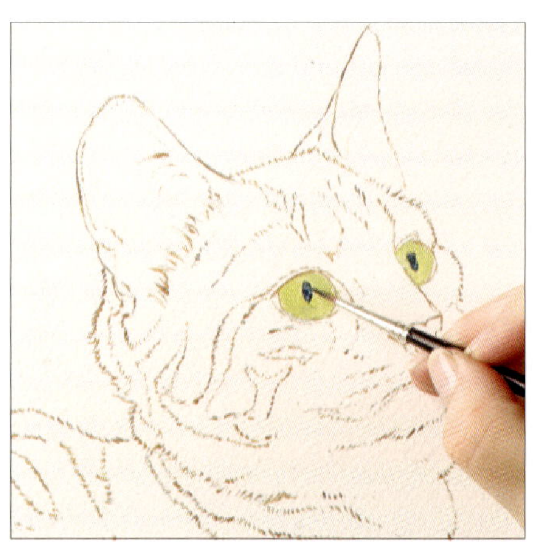

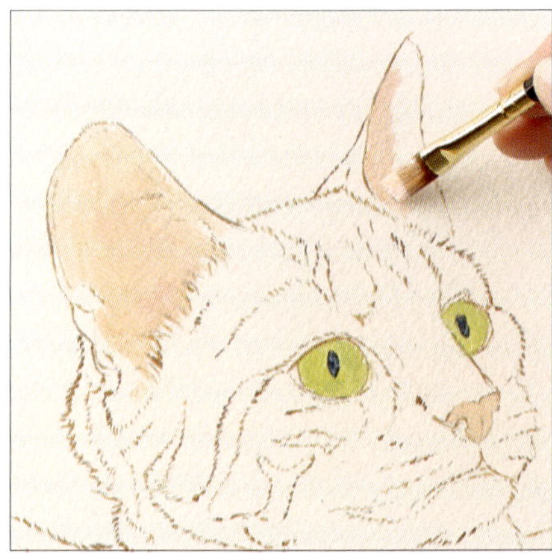

1 Transfer the image to the paper following the instructions on page 9. Outline with raw sienna diluted with a little water, to make it flow more easily, using a size 1 or 3 round brush. Prepare a pale green mix using cadmium yellow, cerulean blue and white. Using a 3mm (⅛in) flat brush, block in the eyes.

2 Prepare a mix using Hooker's green and French ultramarine. Using a size 1 round brush, paint in the pupils of the cat's eyes.

3 Change back to the 3mm (⅛in) flat brush and prepare a very pale peach mix of mostly white with a touch of cadmium red and cadmium yellow and block in the nose. Change to a 6mm (¼in) flat brush and apply the peach colour to the ears. Start working from the centre of each ear and work the colour outwards. Make the colour slightly darker (pinker) towards the centre of the ear. Add white to the peach mix and use this paler colour for the outside edges of the ears.

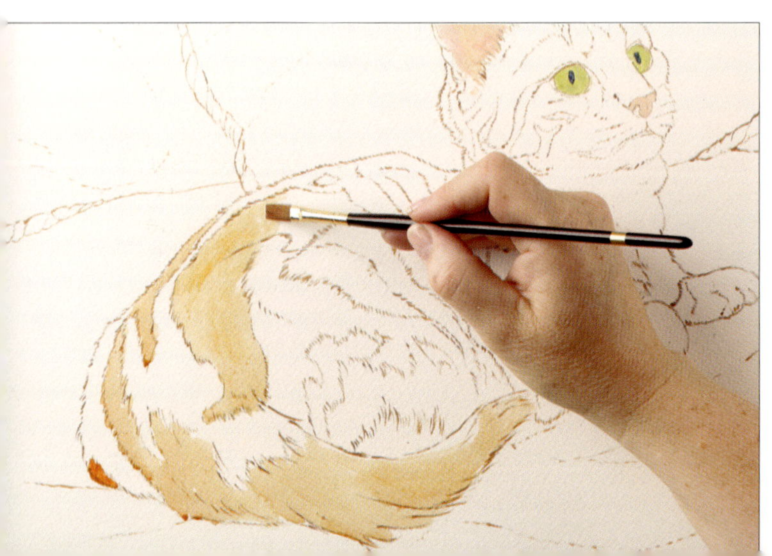

4 Change to a 13mm (½in) flat brush and begin blocking in the fur colours. Prepare a thin ginger-coloured mix using raw sienna with a tiny amount of cadmium red. Paint on the cat's stripes.

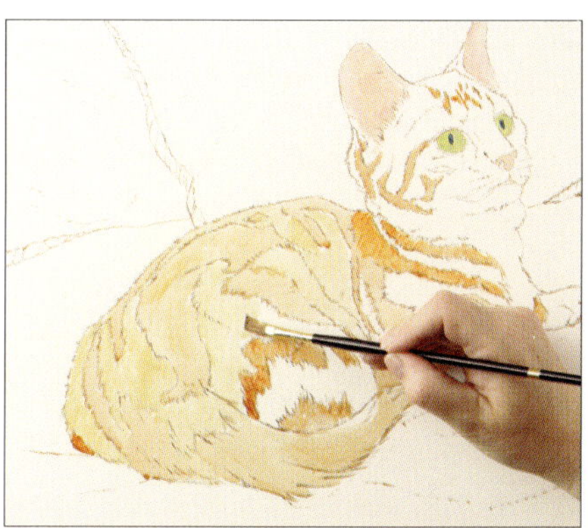

5 Add some burnt sienna to the ginger mix (to make a dark ginger colour) and block in the darker stripes on the cat's body and around his collar.

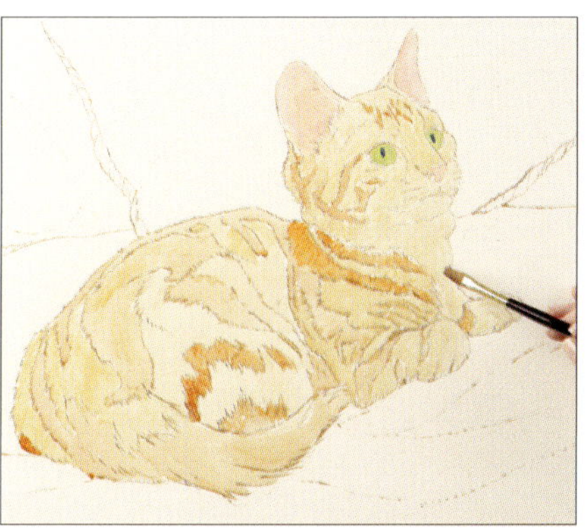

6 Prepare a light ginger colour using a mix of raw umber and white, and block in the remaining stripes on the fur, applying it as a thin wash. Use the flat side of the brush to block in and the edge to apply the paint to finer areas. Add white to the mix to make a paler shade for the head and paws. Add more white for around the mouth and chest area.

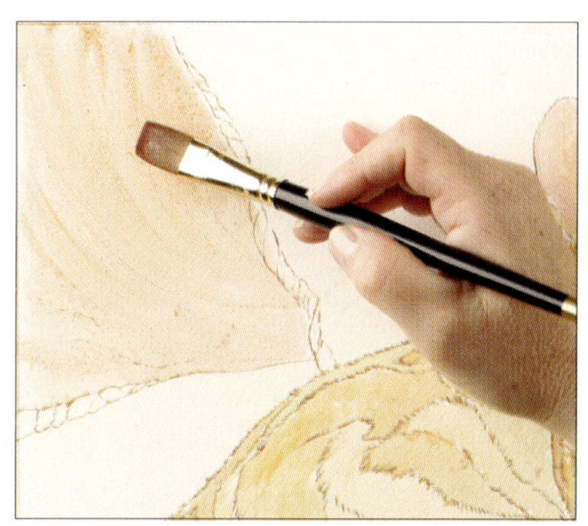

7 Prepare a pool of burnt sienna and a mix of burnt sienna with a touch of French ultramarine. Using a 15mm (⅝in) flat brush, swap between the two mixes to paint in the cushions. Use the mix for the darker areas and apply the colour in curved, sweeping strokes to suggest plumpness in the cushions. Go in darker behind the cat for depth, angling the brushstrokes to suggest the shape of the cushions.

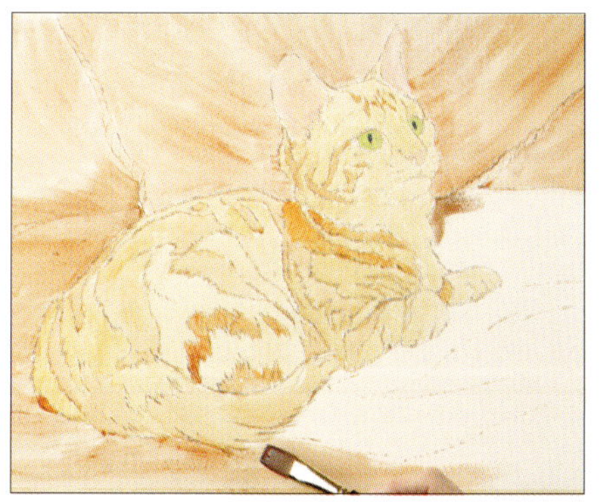

8 Using the burnt sienna and French ultramarine mix, overlap the colour between the drawn lines of the cushions and feather outwards from these lines. Use a burnt sienna wash for the base of the cushion and continue to block in this colour around the cat, keeping the brushstrokes horizontal. Angle your strokes slightly in places to suggest dimples in the cushion.

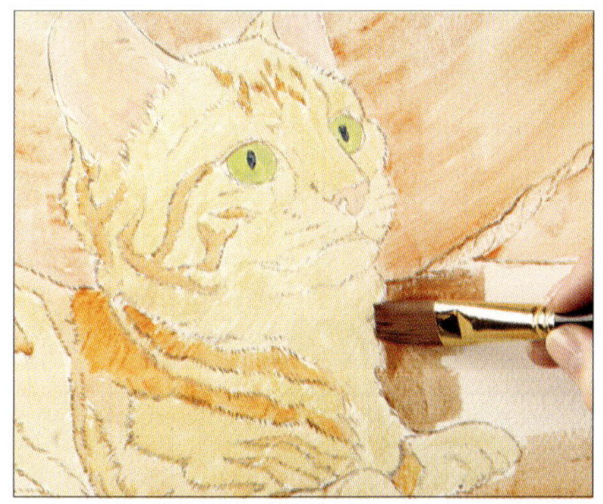

9 Using a stronger preparation of the burnt sienna and French ultramarine mix (rather than a wash), paint from just below the paw up to the cat's chest using sweeping horizontal strokes. The picture should all be blocked in now.

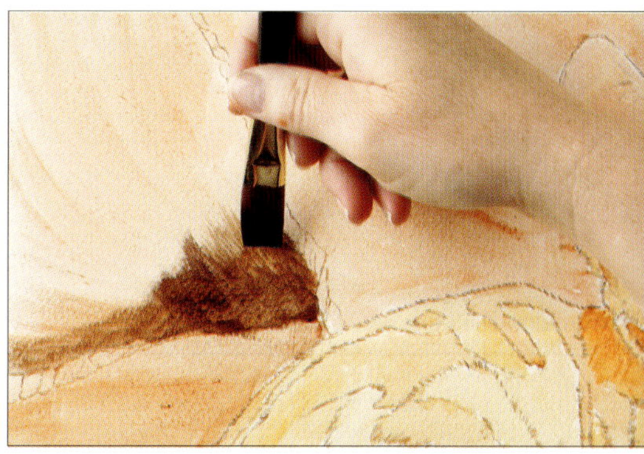

10 Prepare a darker shade of the burnt sienna and French ultramarine mix by adding in a larger proportion of French ultramarine. Use this mix to add shadow into the corners between the cushions.

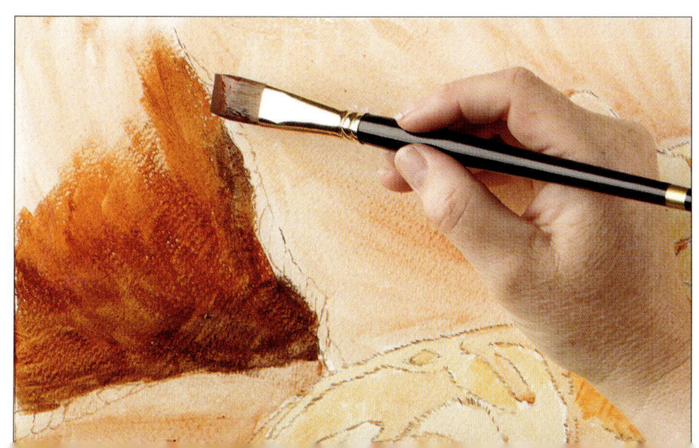

11 Without washing your brush, pick up some neat burnt sienna and blend the colour outwards, allowing the colours to merge together. The colours should be slightly lighter at the top for highlights on the cushion, and darker in the shadowed areas. Repeat this technique for the rest of the background.

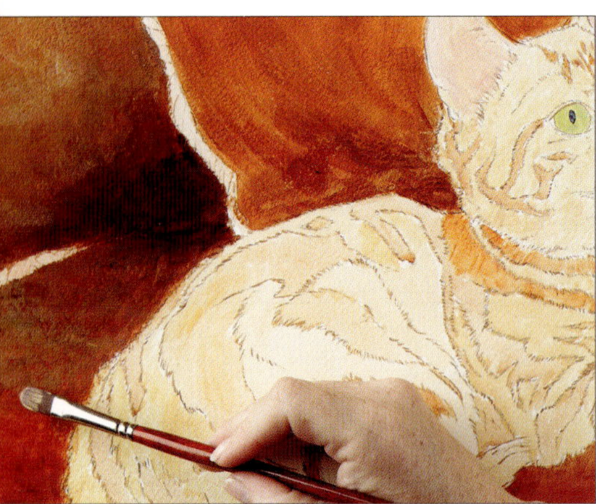

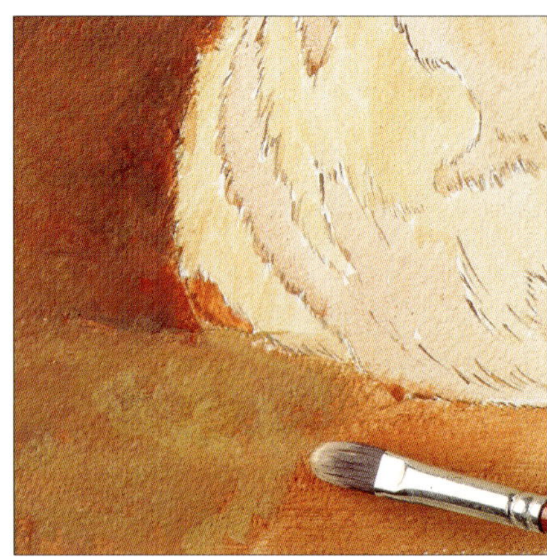

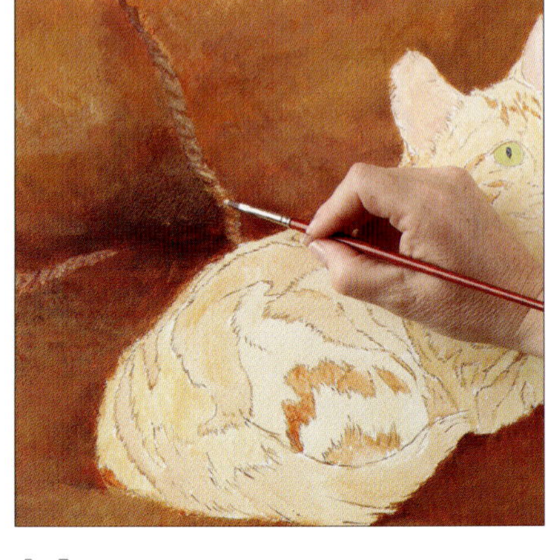

12 Create a light brown mix using raw sienna and white with a touch of deep violet. Using a size 6 filbert brush, apply the colour quite thick and dry to allow the colours underneath to show through on the cushions. For the warmer patches, prepare a warm brown with raw sienna and cadmium yellow. Work up the background using short strokes on the flat of your brush, dabbing on the colour for a slightly textured look. Don't wash your brush as you swap between the two colour mixes.

13 Using short, feathery strokes, blend the colours and make them soft around the tail. Lighten the very dark areas by stippling with the colours used in the previous step. Start dark and gradually work lighter. Continue with this technique around the cat's head, working downwards around the body.

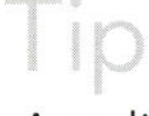

Acrylic paint dries very quickly so you will have to blend between the colours as you go.

14 For the cushion braids: change to a size 2 filbert brush and use the same three colour mixes. Block in the braids with the burnt sienna and French ultramarine mix then apply the light brown mix in short, stippling strokes alternating with the warm brown mix. Use a mix of raw sienna with white for the lighter areas and the highlights, and to describe the weave of the braid. The background should now be completely painted in.

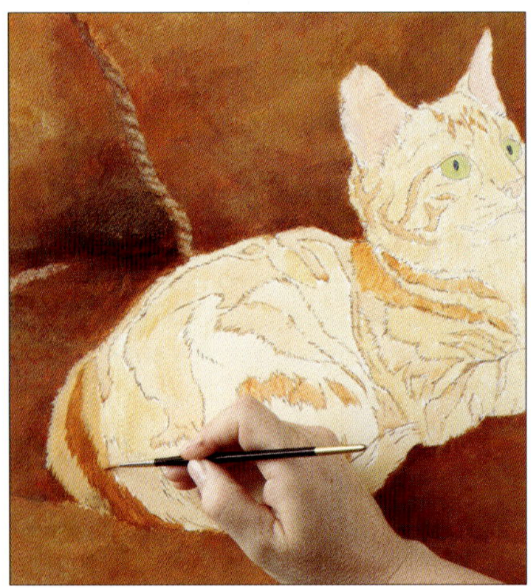

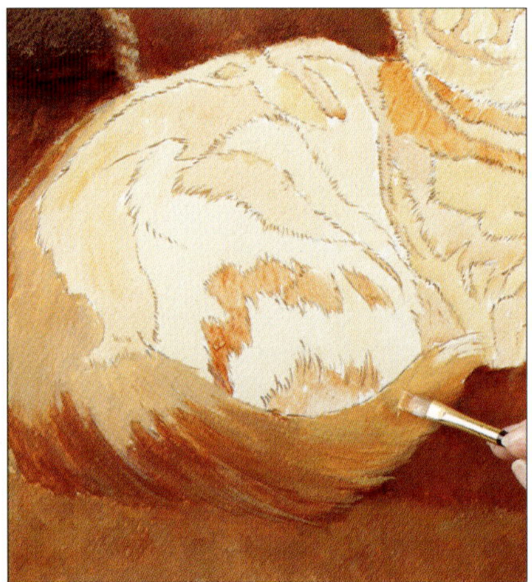

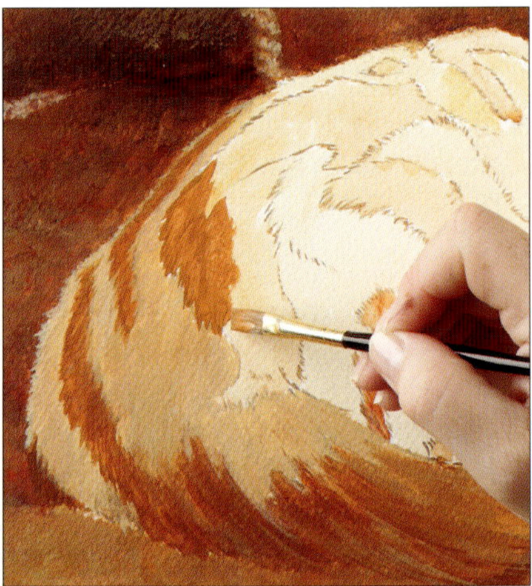

15 Create some more ginger-coloured mixes using raw sienna and white by varying the proportions of each colour. Return to your original ginger mix and using these new mixes and a size 2 round brush, use an 'on-off' stroke to suggest the fur. Work from the edges first with this brush and use a 13mm (½in) flat brush for painting in larger areas of the fur. Alternate your brushstrokes between the ginger mixes.

16 Use burnt sienna, burnt umber and a mix of raw sienna, cadmium red and a touch of deep violet for the darker and shadowed areas on the fur. To take the sharpness out of the dark colours, blend with one of your paler ginger mixes at the edges of each stripe. Be sure to draw your brushstrokes in the same way the fur is laying.

17 Continue to build up the markings on the cat's fur by swapping between the ginger mixes and the colours in step 16, working from the middle of each stripe outwards and pulling the colour outwards. Keep the edges of each stripe jagged to suggest the furry edges and swap between brushes.

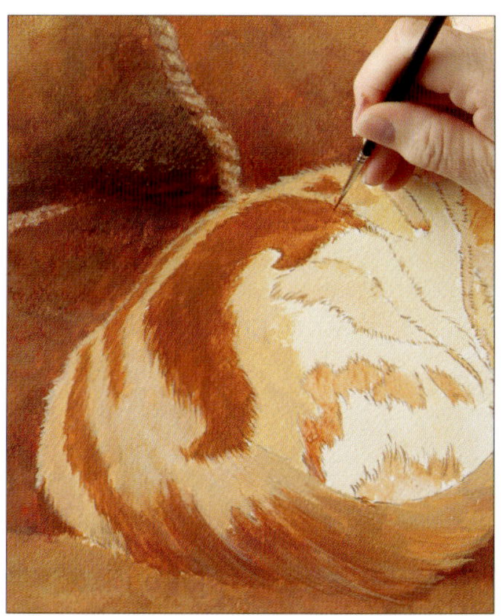
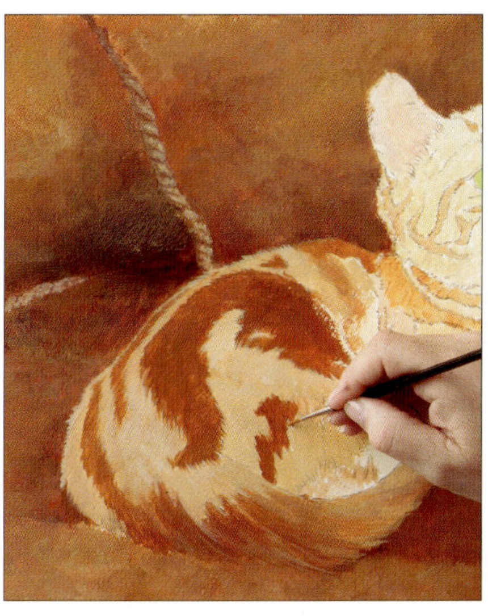
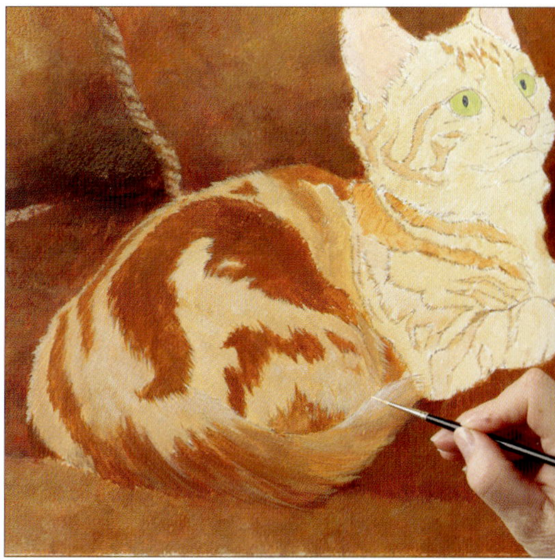

18 Using the size 2 round brush, and a pale ginger mix, paint in a few lighter strokes while the dark fur is still wet. This suggests light fur and also highlights in the dark fur. Work up the tail in the same way.

19 Go back over the first layer of the pale stripes and, using a lighter mix, feather the edges into the darker stripes to create the illusion of fur. Continue to work up the stripes on the fur using this technique. It does not matter if some stripes are thicker and others are thinner.

20 Work down the middle section of the cat using the same technique to create the illusion of fur. Add pure white for the highlights to the tail.

Tip

Use one brush loaded with the lighter stripe colour and the other with the darker colour so that you don't have to keep washing your brush when you switch between the mixes.

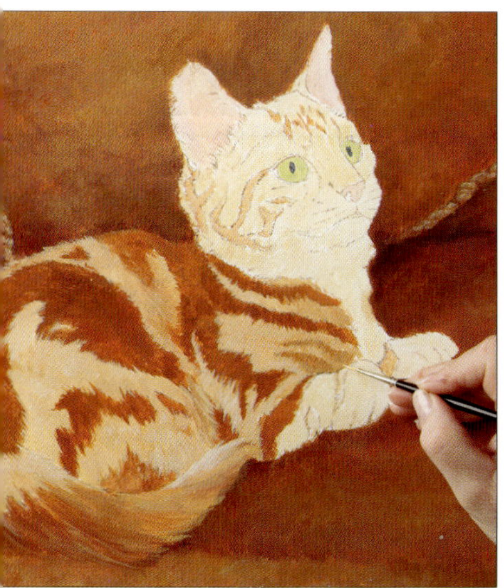
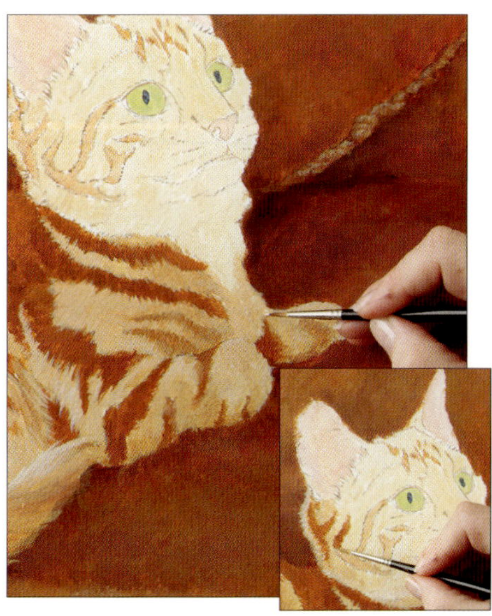
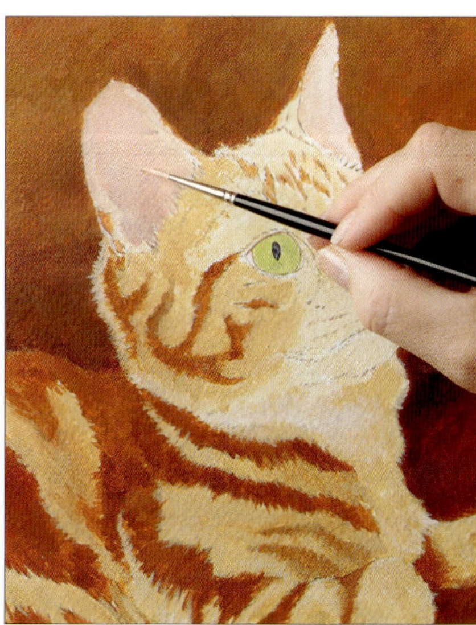

21 Use a size 2 round brush on the thin stripes, working from the middle of the stripe outwards. Work up the rest of the thin stripes on the cat's neck. Blend your stripe colours to achieve a mid-tone ginger and paint in the two stripes on the front of the chest in this colour using the size 2 round brush.

22 Next, work on the paws using the same technique with the mid-tone ginger mix, the lighter ginger mixes and the original ginger mix. Lighten the paws at the front. Start to paint in the dark stripes on the face and between the stripes paint in varying pale shades of ginger using your mixes from step 15.

23 For the ears, prepare a pale pink colour by mixing cadmium red and white with a little of the pale ginger mix. Mix in a touch of cobalt blue to add shadow to the centre of the ear. Add a little more white to the pink to make a paler colour to paint in the outside edges of the ears.

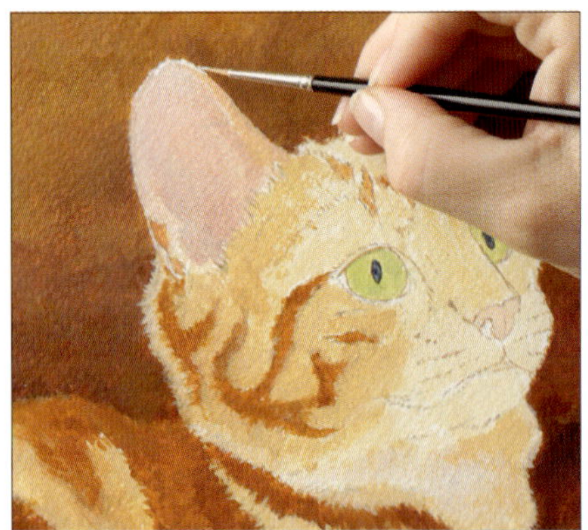

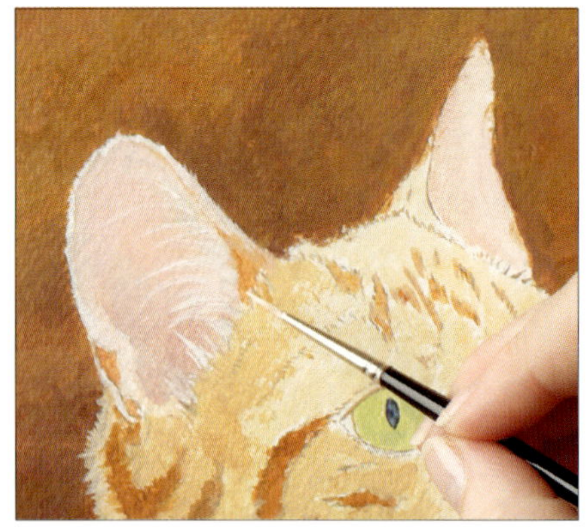

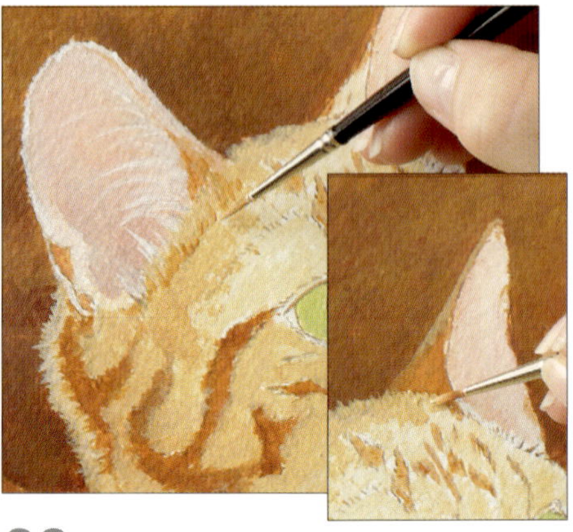

24 Change to a size 1 round brush and, using little dotting actions, stipple the brush around the tip and outside edge of the ear. This will make it stand out from the background and suggest strands of hair. Blend the white with the pale ginger mix for the hairs at the base of and inside the ears.

25 Starting at the front base of the ear, use fine, sweeping strokes to suggest hairs, using pure white. Sweep and lift your brush off to create tapered strokes.

26 Using the pale ginger colour, paint on the patch in front of the nearest ear to mark its edge. Apply this pale mix to the back of the furthest ear and then go in darker at the base using the mid-tone ginger mix. The ears should both be darkest at the base and lightest at the tip. Repeat steps 24–25 for the furthest ear.

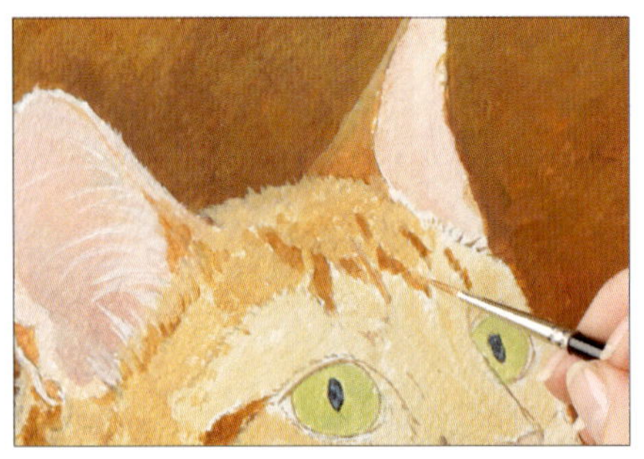

27 For the cat's head: stipple and blend in various tones of the pale and mid-tone ginger fur colours in and around the dark markings. Be sure not to cover these markings, so apply the paint quite thinly so that they still show through. Use the paler mixes around the eye and eyebrow area.

Tip

Change the direction of your brushstrokes to match the direction of the fur for a more realistic effect.

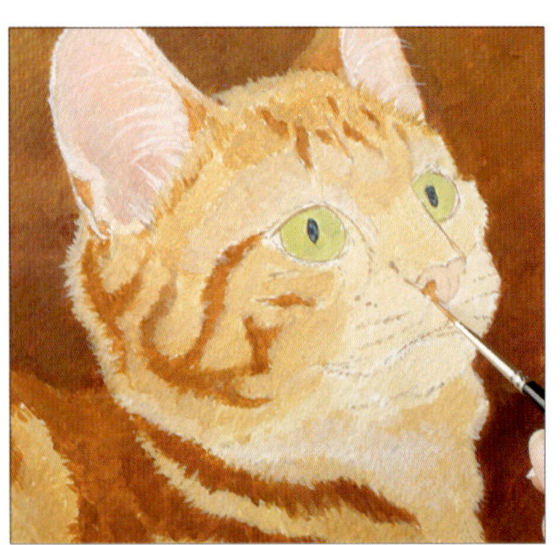

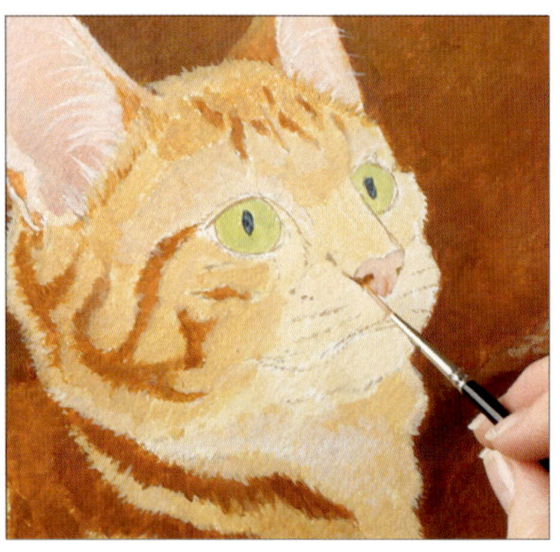

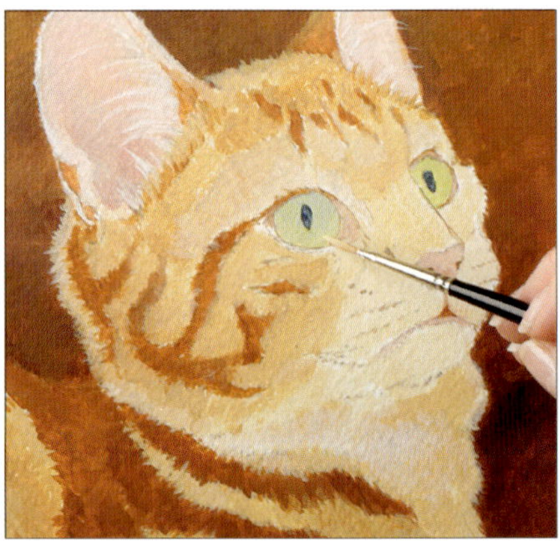

28 Mark in the nostril in burnt sienna and then add a touch more cobalt blue to the pink ear colour, to make a darker pink, and apply a touch of this to the bottom of the nose. Take a little burnt umber and blend this to the nostril area to add in some darkness.

29 Paint in the mouth using the pink ear colour, painting a slightly stronger pink towards the centre of the mouth by adding a touch of burnt sienna and blending.

30 Prepare a mix of raw sienna with a tiny touch of deep violet. Outline the top of the eye and draw the brush down the line of the nose, increasing the violet colour in the mix slightly. Repeat for the other eye.

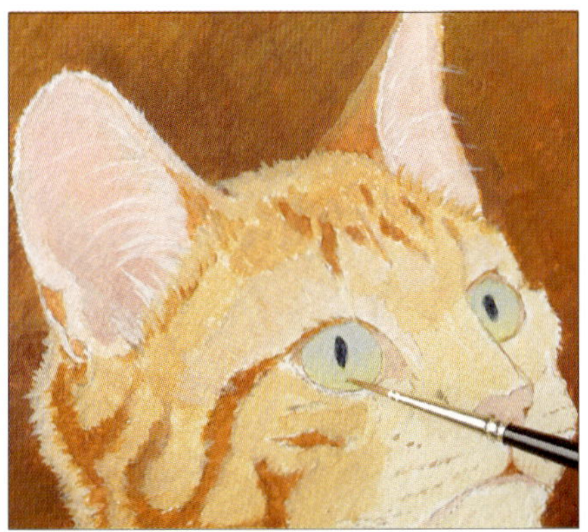

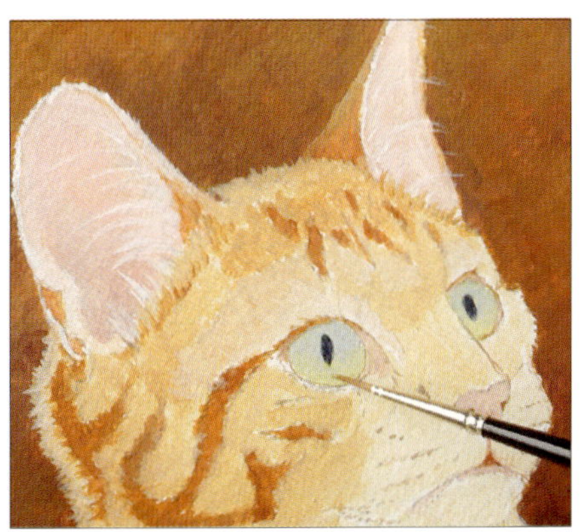

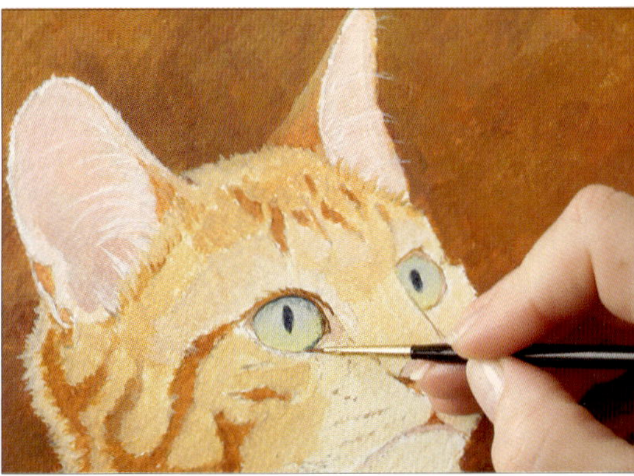

31 Using varying proportions of cerulean blue, cadmium yellow and white, prepare two mixes; one blue-green and one yellow-green. Paint the bluer mix towards the top of the eye, and the yellow-green mix towards the bottom. Repeat for the other eye.

32 Return to your original mix of Hooker's green and French ultramarine (step 2) and use this mix to strengthen the colour in the pupils of each eye. Prepare a fluid mix of cobalt blue and white, and paint another layer along the top of each eye and on the yellow-green colour on the bottom.

33 Return to the raw sienna and deep violet mix (step 30), and subtly define the inside edge of the eye, then outline just below this with the Hooker's green and French ultramarine mix for shadow. Using an almost pure white mix, with only a tiny touch of raw sienna, touch on some highlights on the lower eyelid.

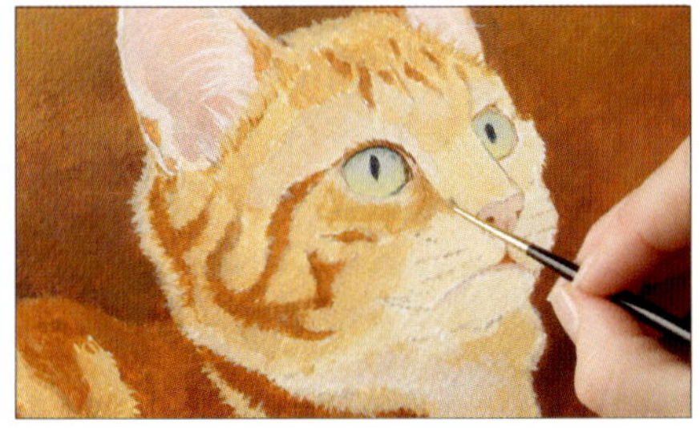

34 Return to your mid-tone ginger mix and paint into the corner of each eye to give the face some form and shape. Using a 3mm (⅛in) flat brush, paint short strokes to suggest fur on the nose and around it using a pale ginger mix.

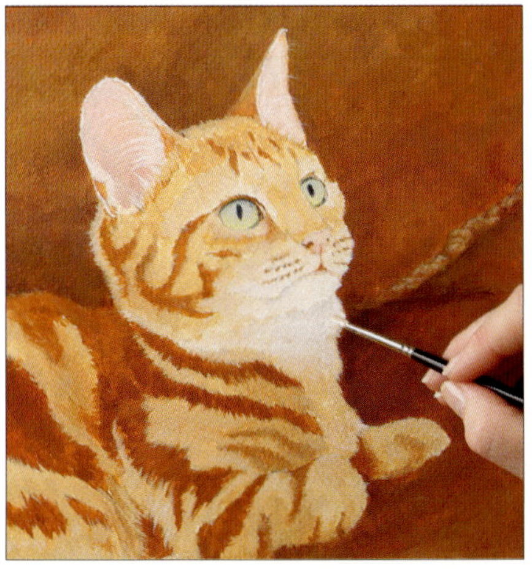

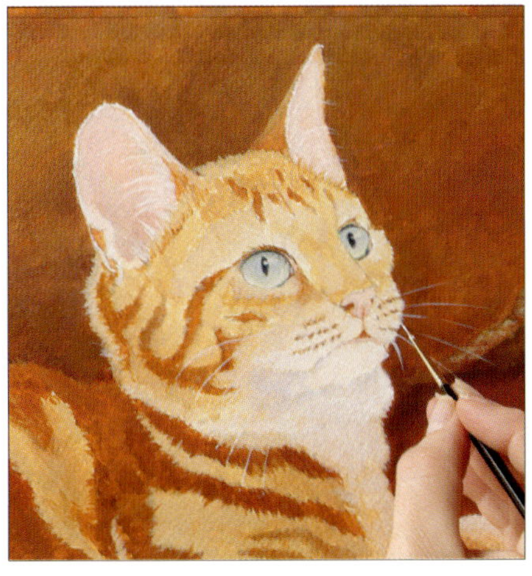

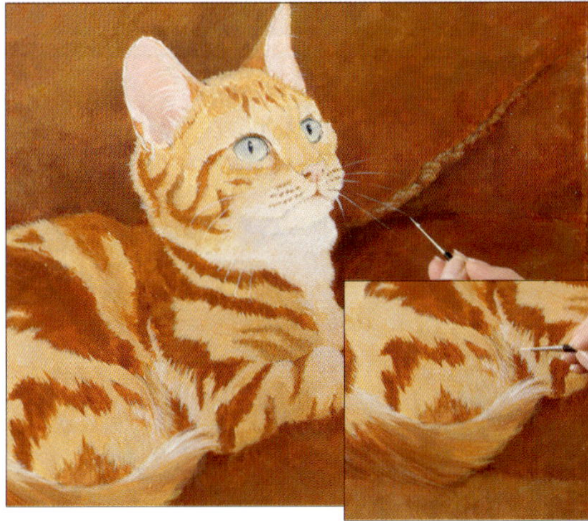

35 Change to the 6mm (¼in) flat brush and paint fur on to the chin in white paint. Add a touch of cobalt blue to the white mix and paint directly below the chin for shadow.

36 Change to a size 1 round brush and dot in the whisker follicles using a slightly darker raw sienna and deep violet mix. Work between the follicles with the palest ginger mix and use short strokes to suggest fur. Take a small amount of fluid white and add highlights to the eyes.

37 Use a size 3 round brush for the whiskers. Take some fairly fluid white paint (but not transparent) and use sweeping brushstrokes from each follicle outwards. Try to paint each whisker in one, sweeping stroke. Vary between using a size 1 and a size 3 round brush and add in highlights to the fur as you see fit across the painting.

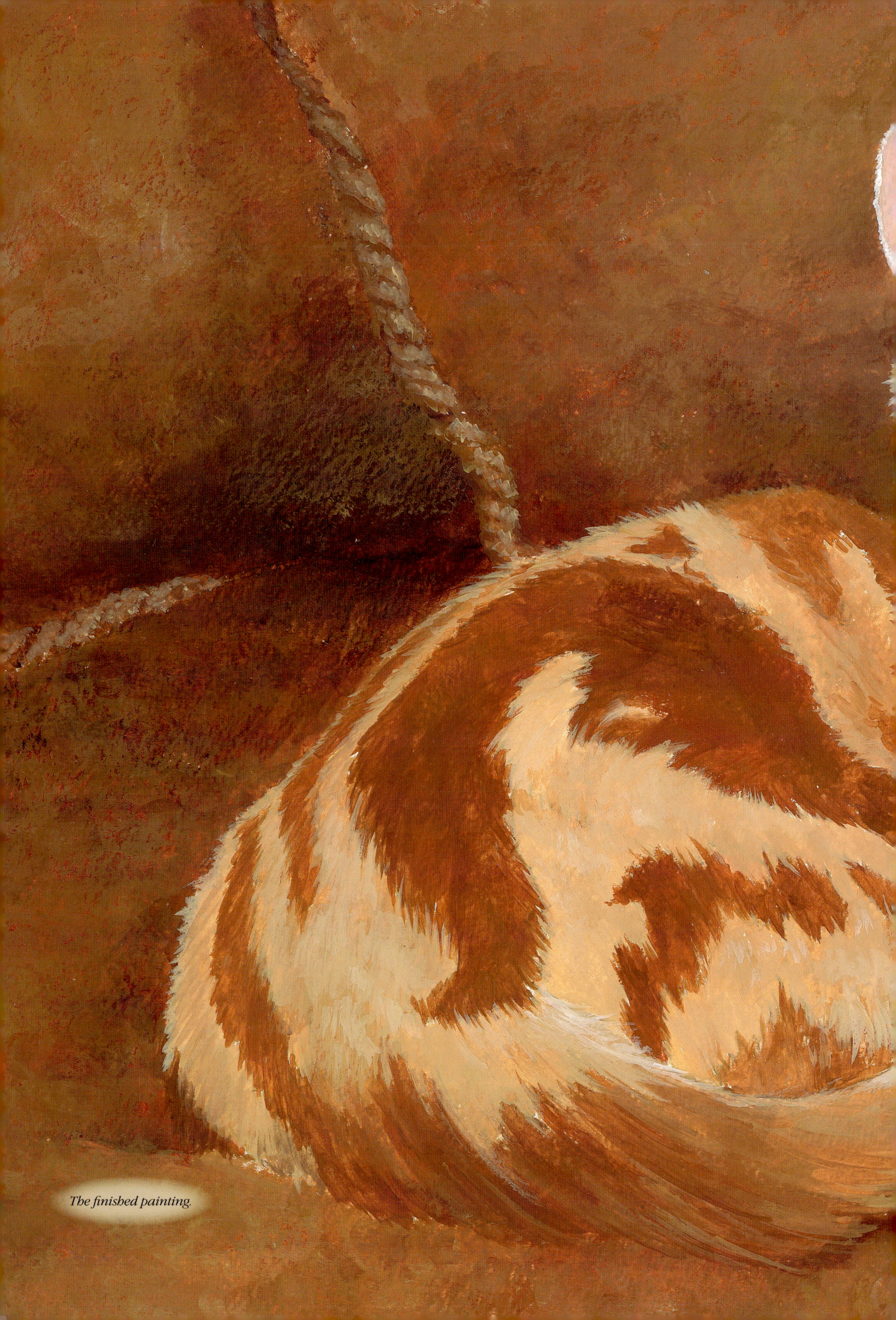

The finished painting.

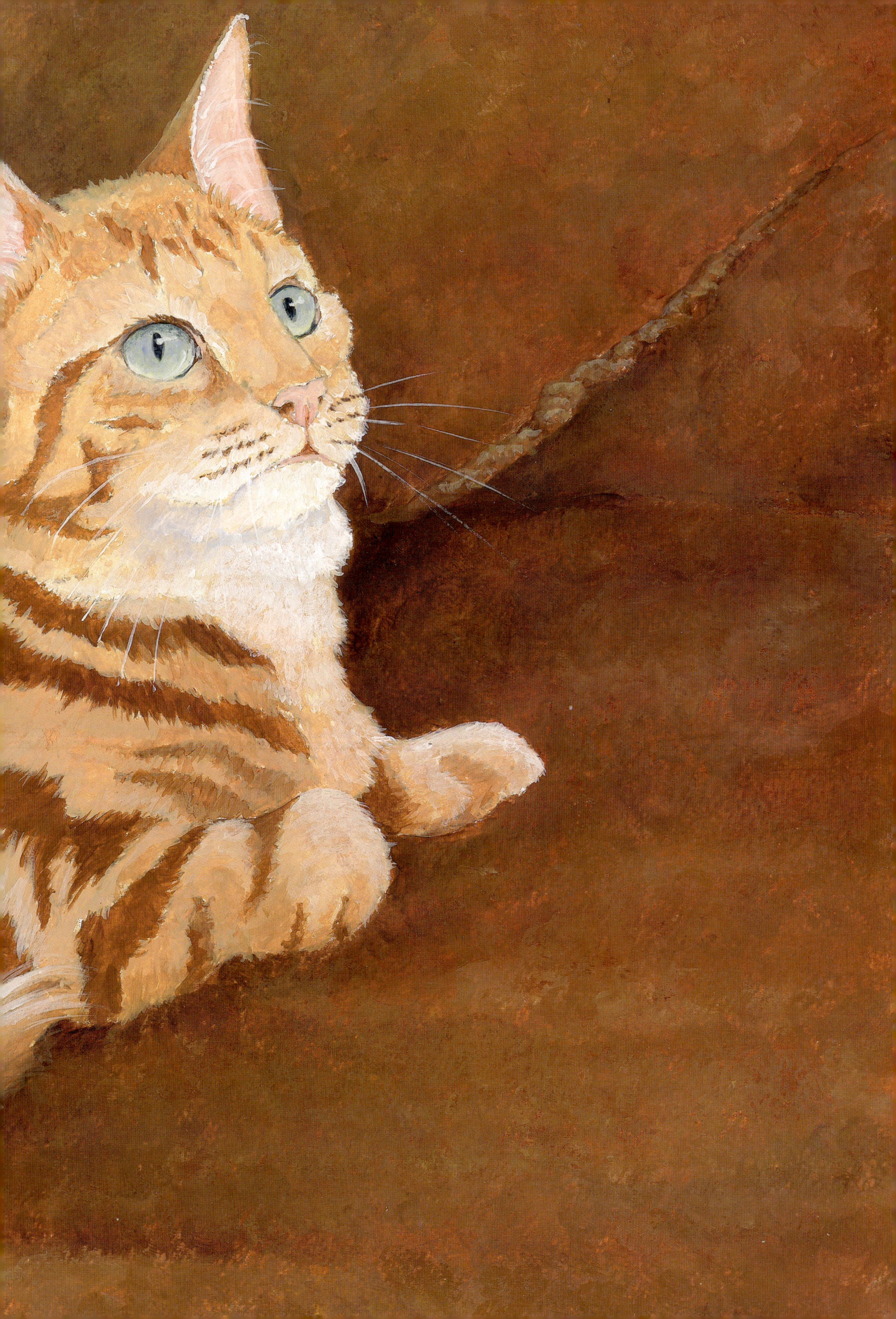

Elegant Profile

What a handsome feline. I like the strong sunlight in this picture which highlights lots of interesting ruffles in the fur and intensifies the golden orange of the eye. It made me think of Ra, the Egyptian sun god. Here I have used strong tonal contrast to portray the bright light. The large scale of this painting makes it ideal for practising cat's eyes; try repeating this one using the different eye colours from the other demonstrations.

Tip

To blend acrylic paint, work wet into wet. If you find yourself lifting paint off when you are blending, stop, let it dry and then work back over the area.

You will need

300gsm (140lb) Rough or Not watercolour paper

Colours: raw sienna, cadmium red, cadmium yellow, titanium white, cobalt blue, French ultramarine, burnt umber, yellow ochre, burnt sienna, Hooker's green

Brushes: size 1 round, size 2 round, size 3 round, size 4 round, 3mm (⅛in) flat, 6mm (¼in) flat, 15mm (⅝in) flat, size 2 filbert

Eraser

Spray bottle

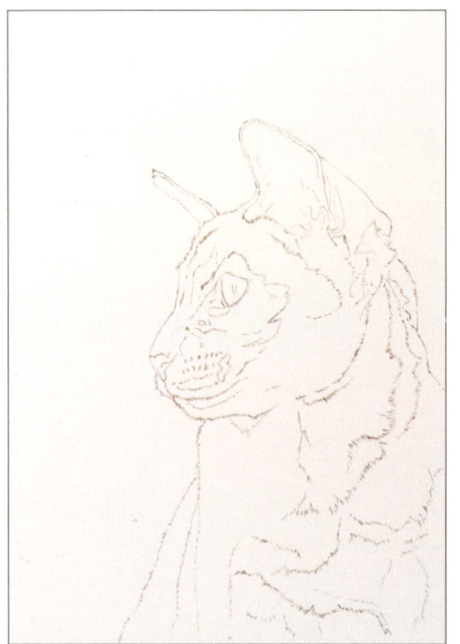

1 Transfer tracing 2 on to watercolour paper as shown on page 9. Outline the cat with raw sienna, diluted to the consistency of ink, using a size 1 or a size 3 round brush.

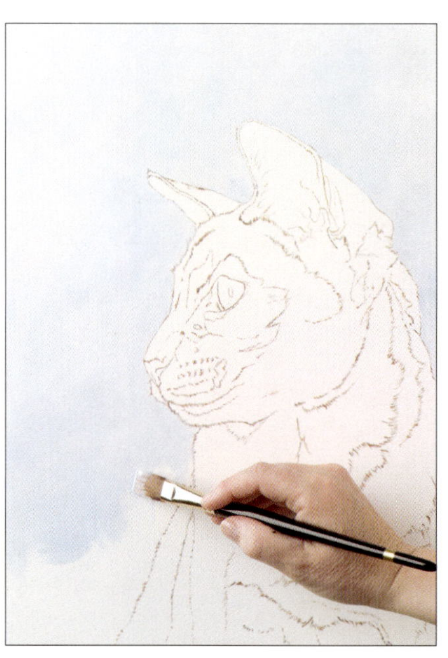

2 Moisten your paper by spraying it lightly with water. Using the 15mm (⅝in) flat brush make strokes back and forth over the background with a mix of cobalt blue and white. Be sure to avoid going over the outlining on the cat's ears. Cover the entire background, making it lighter at the top and gradually becoming darker towards the bottom.

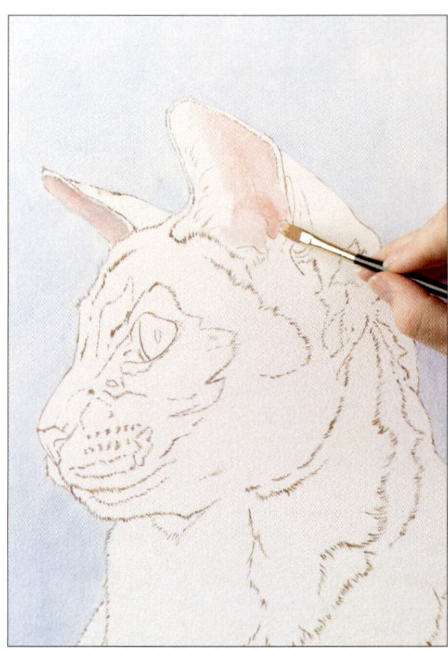

3 Use the 6mm (¼in) flat brush for the ears. Prepare a mix of white, cadmium red, cadmium yellow and a tiny touch of cobalt blue. Paint the insides of the ears, making them paler towards the outside edge.

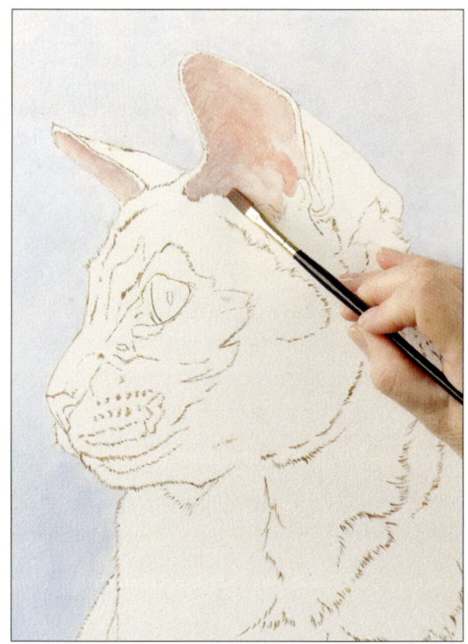
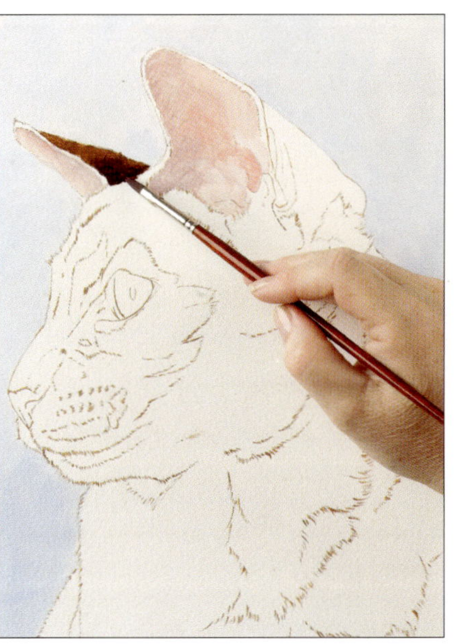
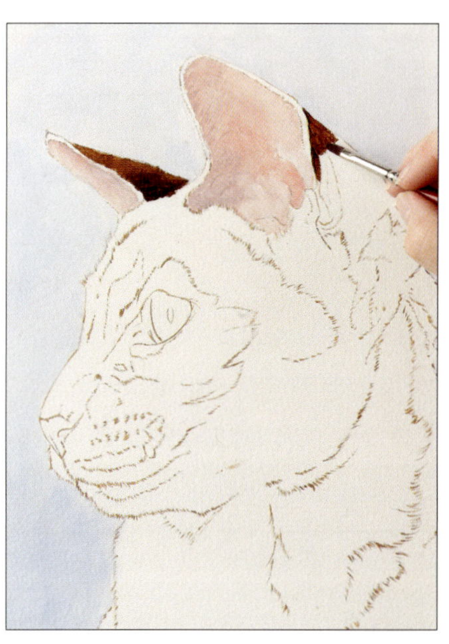

4 Add a touch more cobalt blue to the pink ear mix to make a pink-lilac shade and paint a little on the left of the nearest inner ear for depth and shadow. Add white to the paler edges.

5 Make a brown mix from cadmium red, cadmium yellow and French ultramarine. Apply this colour to the ears and blend with burnt umber, working darker towards the base of the ear. You may want to swap to a size 2 filbert brush to stipple and blend in the burnt umber.

6 Using a size 2 filbert and burnt umber, pick out the ear pocket on the nearest ear.

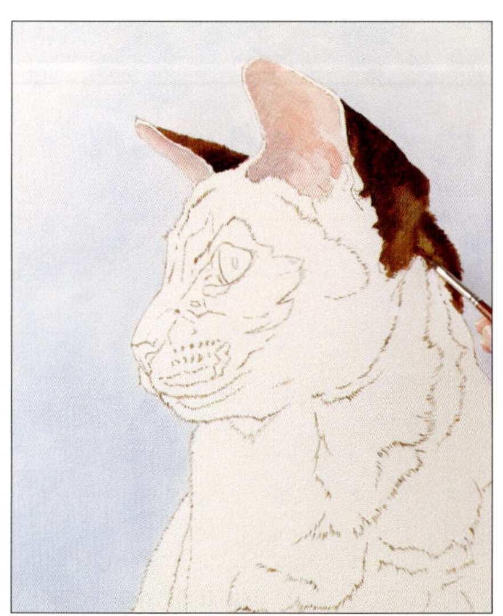
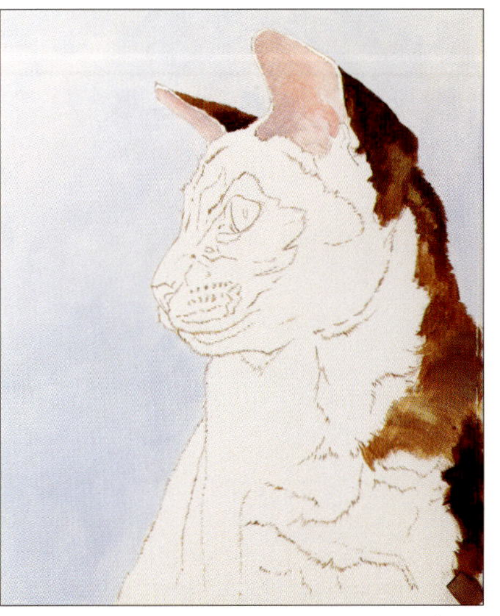
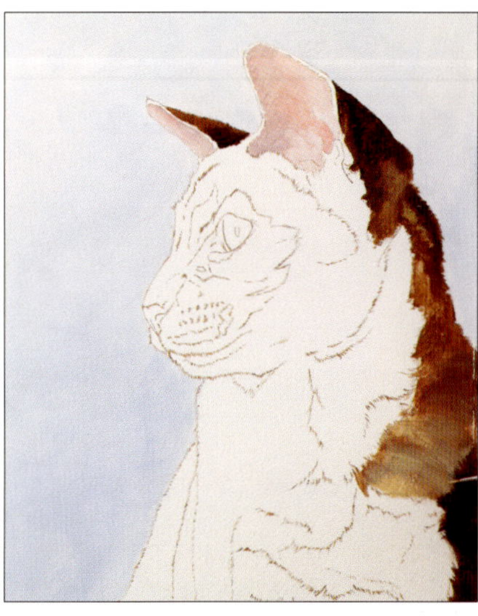

7 Pick up some of the brown mix (step 5) and work your way down the ear from the tip and blend it with burnt umber to make a dark brown. Add some yellow ochre into the brown mix to make a light brown colour and again, work down the ear, blending into the previous brown shades.

8 Swap to a 15mm (⅝in) flat brush and work down the back of the cat's fur using the brown and a cream colour from a mix of yellow ochre and white. Blend the colours together in flat sweeping strokes. Apply burnt umber down the right side of the cat to suggest shadow.

9 Apply more of the cream mix towards the middle of the cat's body. Pull out the colour using a size 2 round brush to create a furry edge.

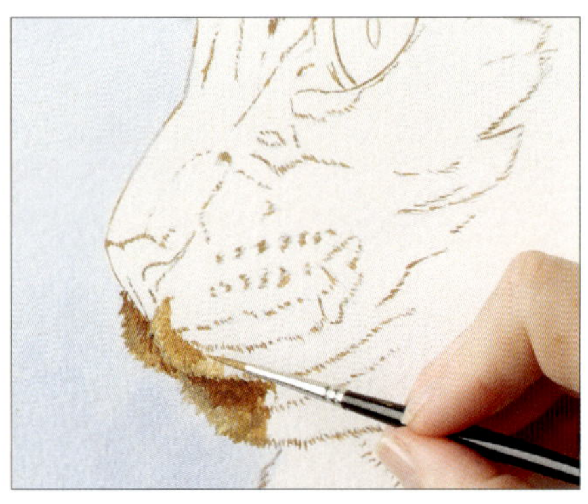

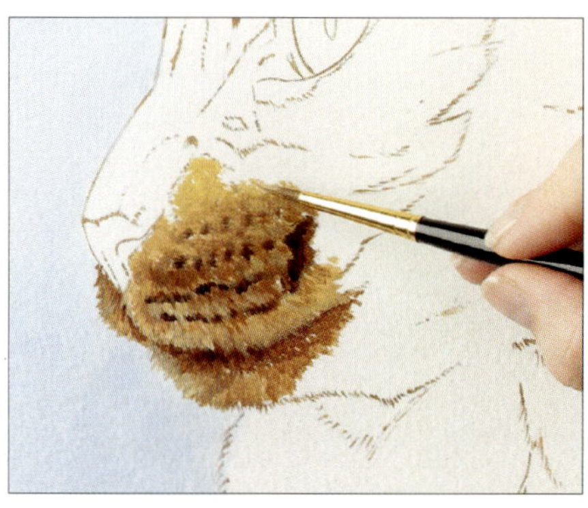

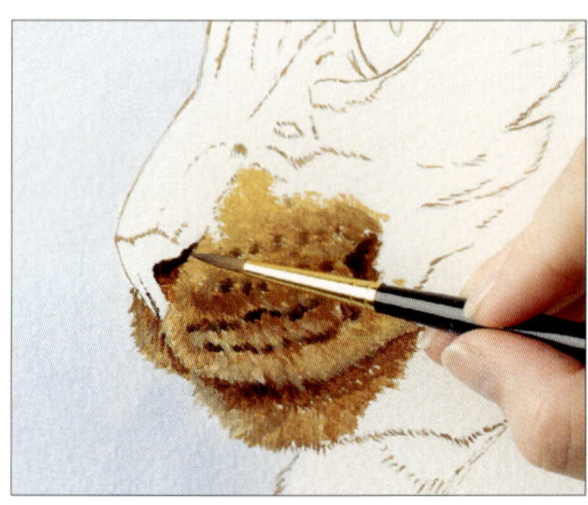

10 Paint on the lips starting with the cream mix. Gradually make the colour darker towards the far edge of the lip using the light brown mix and blending so that it becomes a caramel colour. Apply in a darker shade just under the lip for shadow and blend with the caramel colour to produce a light and dark contrast. Outline the mouth in this darker shade of the original brown mix.

11 Change to a size 4 round brush and using the darker shade of the brown mix, use short brushstrokes to work up the whisker follicles and dark patches on the muzzle. Alternate between the mixes in step 10 with short, on-off strokes, overlapping them to create the illusion of fur. Towards the top of the muzzle at the side of the cat's nose, add a touch of yellow ochre and blend it into the caramel colour.

12 Work up the nose, starting with the nostril in burnt umber and working down into burnt sienna to add warmth.

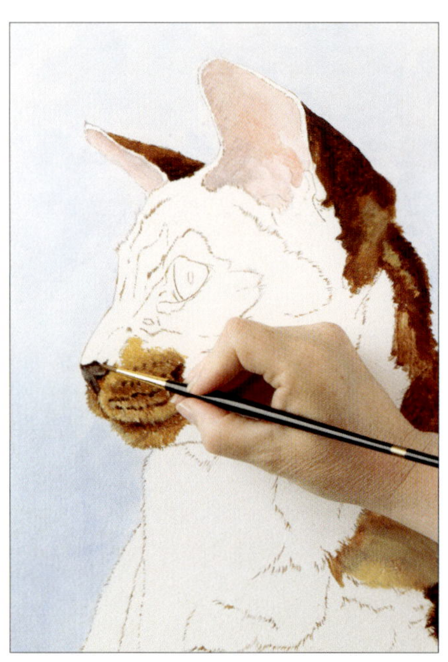

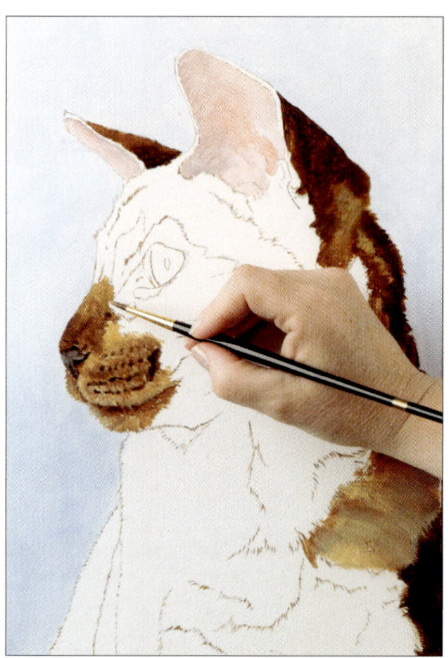

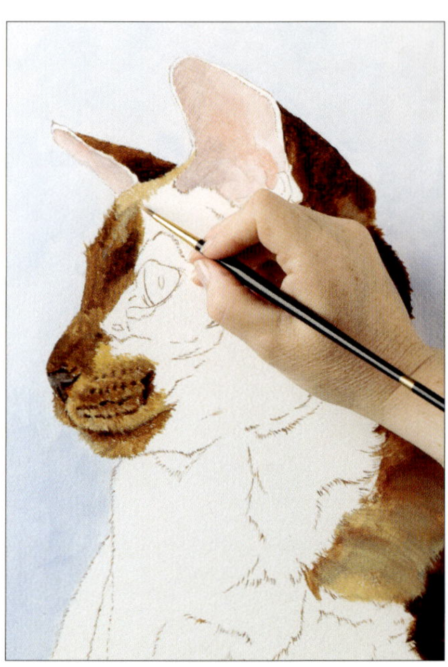

13 Apply a thin wash of burnt umber to the nose and stipple on a grey-brown mix: burnt umber with cobalt blue and white. Use more burnt umber towards the top of the nose to add form.

14 Using the mixes from step 10, stipple from the tip of the nose upwards. This technique gives the impression of very short fur. Use burnt umber for the darker, shadowed areas, the pale brown and caramel shades for the main tone and cream for the light areas. The nose becomes lighter towards the top, near the forehead.

15 As you work towards the forehead, use slightly longer strokes as the fur is longer here. Swap between your colours frequently and work it up in this way rather than doing large areas in one block of colour. Add a little of the cream mix into the pale caramel colours and use short, on-off strokes to block in the crown between the ears.

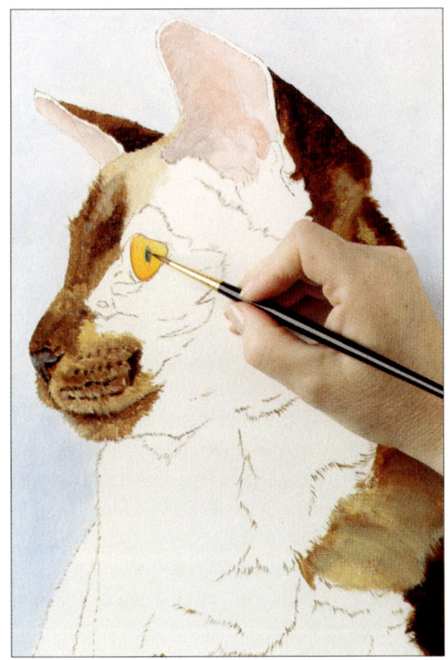

16 Prepare an orange base colour for the eye using cadmium yellow and cadmium red, and a colour for the pupil from French ultramarine and Hooker's green. Paint the eye.

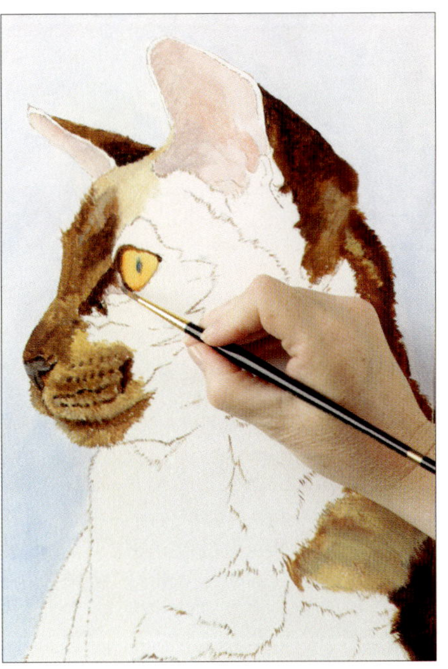

17 Working under the eye, touch some burnt umber into the corner to create a shadowed effect. Pick up some of the pink-lilac mix and dot this into the corner of the eye and blend with the burnt umber. Use your mid-caramel shades around the eyes in short, stippling strokes to create the illusion of fur. Use your lightest shades closest to the eye.

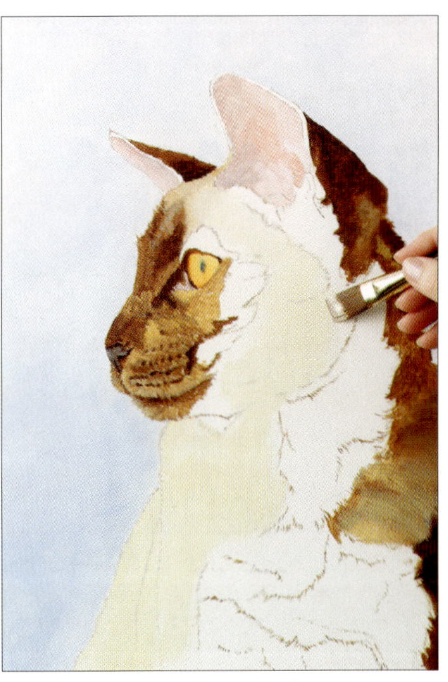

18 Change to a 15mm (⅝in) flat brush and block in a base colour of the cream mix on the neck and chest. Work this base colour up and around the face. This helps you to see where the lightest tones will be when you come to work up the body fur.

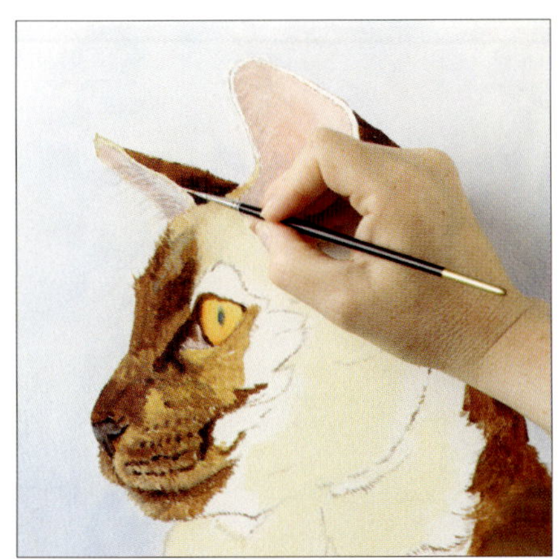

19 Working now on the furthest ear, darken the colours. Use the lilac-pink mix inside the ear and a light caramel shade to dot highlights on to the edge of the ear.

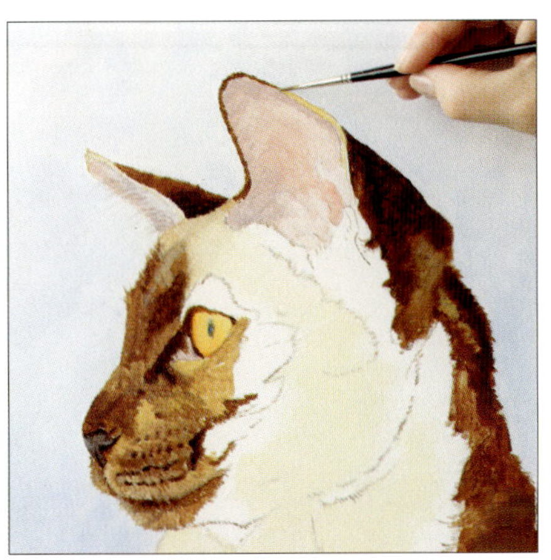

20 Change to a size 1 round brush and, using the grey-brown mix and light sweeping strokes, add fluffy hair to the pink insides of the cat's ears, working from the base outwards. Repeat this technique with white paint and stipple the base of these hairs, close to the edge of the ear. Repeat steps 19 and 20 for the other ear and edge each ear in burnt umber.

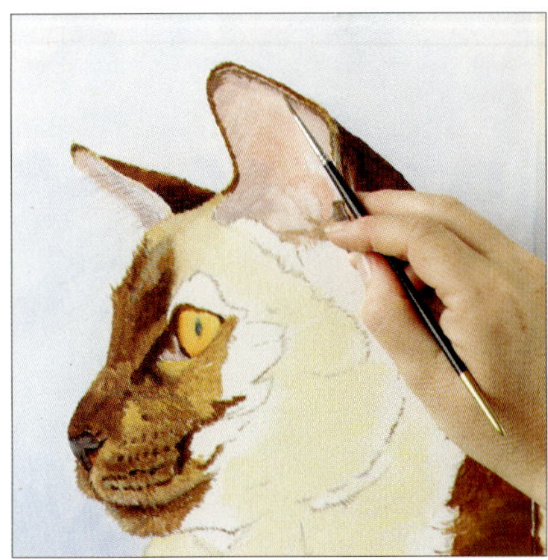

21 Take the grey-brown mix and add highlights to the foreground ear. Add a line of lilac-pink between the brown shades on each ear. Take some white and add in a touch of cobalt blue and use this mix to add in a few highlights on the pink of the ear.

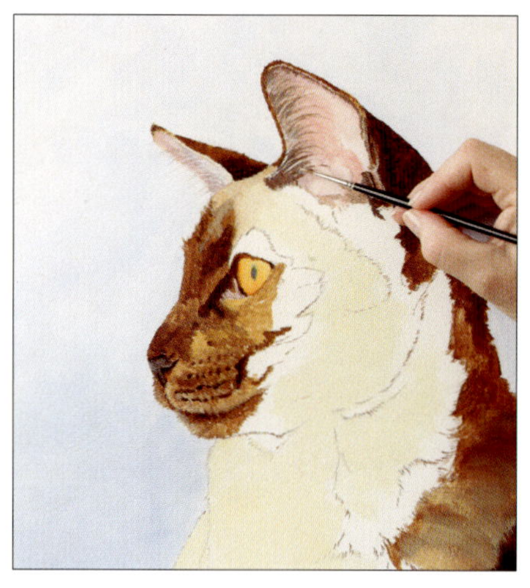

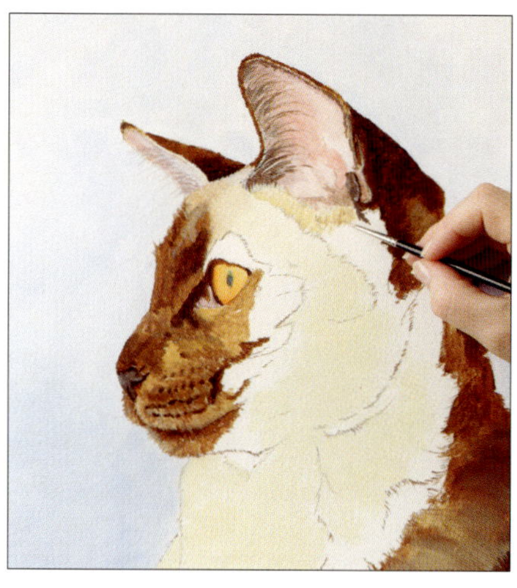

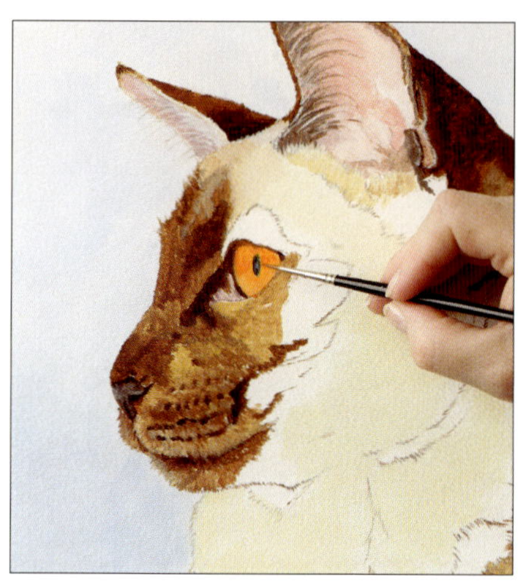

22 Use three mixes; the pink ear colour, the grey-brown mix and white, and alternate between them, working into the base of each ear to add definition. Stipple each colour in and feather your brushstrokes to look like fur. Take your cream mix and add in a few sweeping hairs to the left at the base of the ear.

23 Add more yellow ochre to the cream mix and build up another layer of short, sweeping brushstrokes. Move across the base of the ear using a pale caramel colour.

24 Return to the cat's eye and strengthen the orange colour. Whilst it is still moist, add the cream mix along the bottom and up the right side of the eye. Change to a size 1 round brush and strengthen the pupil colour.

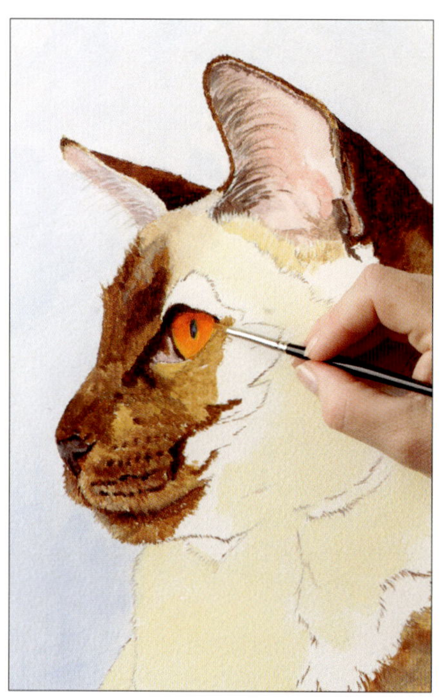

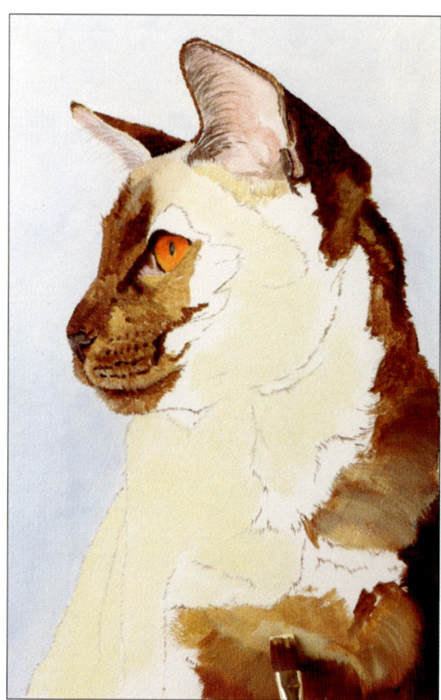

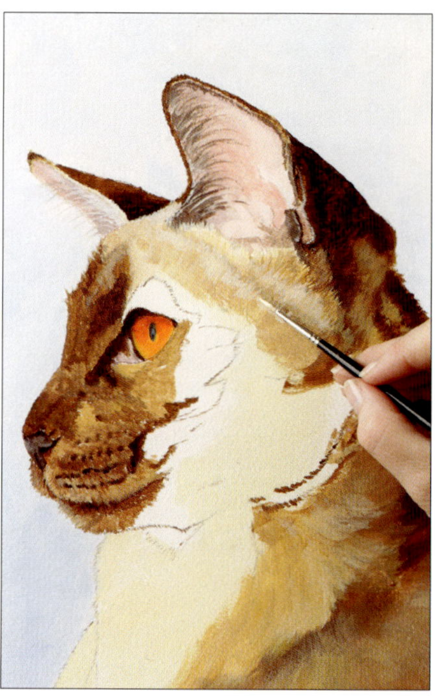

25 Prepare a dark brown mix using burnt umber and French ultramarine. Apply it to the top of the eyebrow, and while still moist, add some burnt sienna to the top of the eye and blend. This gives the eye some shadow.

26 Working from the bottom up, using the 15mm (⅝in) flat brush, block in the rest of the fur using the caramel mixes. While the caramel shades are still moist, use a size 2 round brush to pull out some of the colour using the brown shades to give the impression of fluffy fur.

27 Use a size 2 round brush to add fine, feathery strokes around the head and face in light colours (caramels, creams and white).

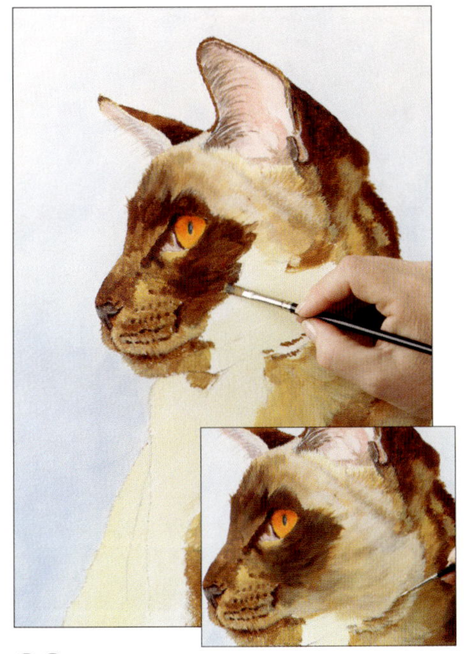

28 Change to a 6mm (¼in) flat brush to paint on the dark eye patch in burnt umber, and re-work the dark fur on the head and around the face. Apply lighter colours to the head again and blend with the dark shades, feathering, to create the fur-like appearance.

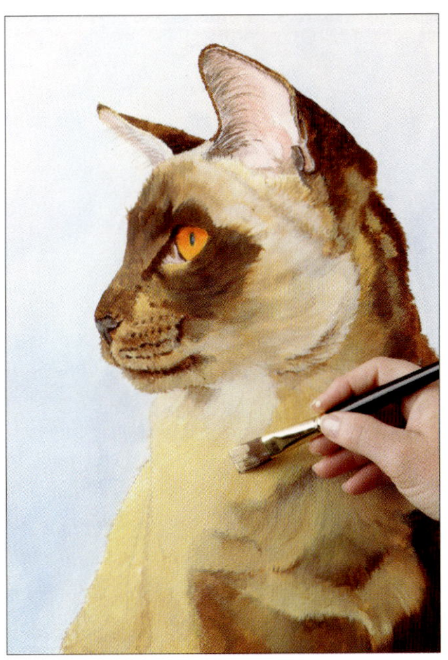

29 Continue with this technique for the caramel-coloured fur, working from right to left, gradually getting lighter towards the left – the lighter side of the cat. Feather the lighter caramel colour into the darker brown colour on the right side. Blend and soften the colours into each other.

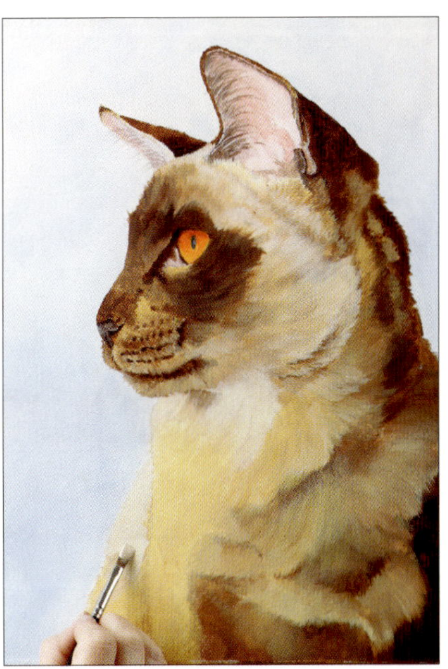

30 Continue to work up the light areas with two cream mixes: white with cadmium yellow and white with yellow ochre. Change to the size 2 round brush to define the edges and to add in more detail. Add the cadmium yellow and white mix under the chin, and then add a light caramel shade to create some shadow.

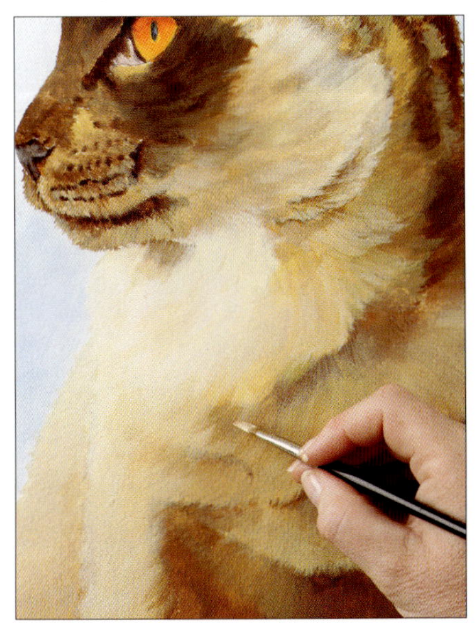

31 Redefine the edges of the varying colours of fur with a mid-caramel shade using the 6mm (¼in) flat brush along the tracing lines in broken lines. Block in using the light caramel mix using a 15mm (⅝in) flat brush. Be sure to overlap where you've been before to keep the edges soft.

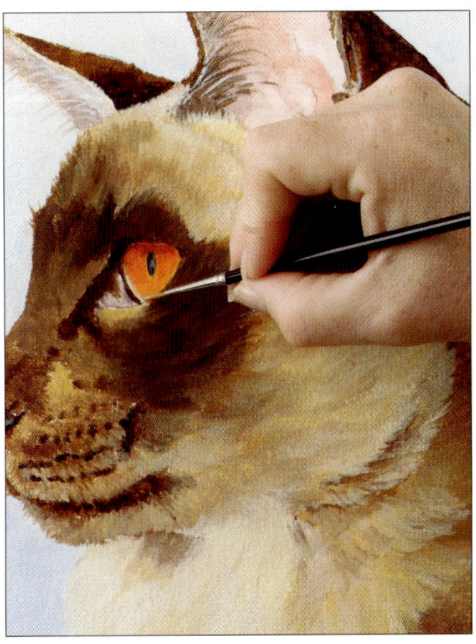

32 Take a size 1 brush and work up the eye by applying some raw sienna to the top and blend it into the orange. Define the edge of the eyeball using pure white on the left.

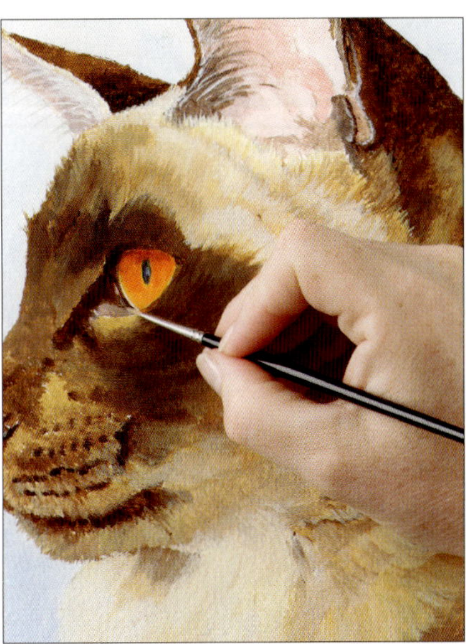

33 Take the pink-lilac ear colour, mix it with the grey-brown and work it in the inside corner of the eye. Use it to refine the shape of the inner eye corner and lower lid.

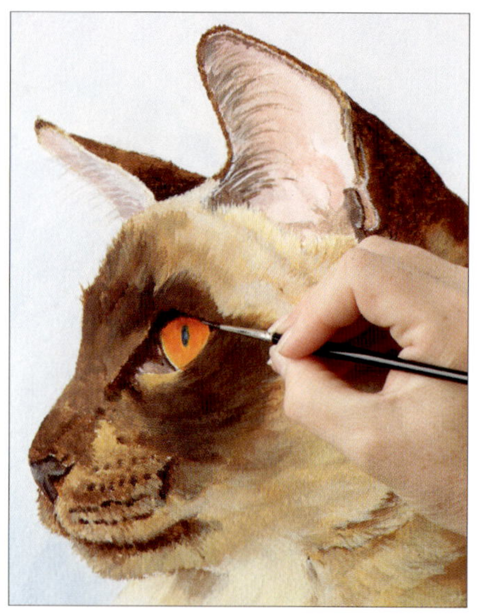 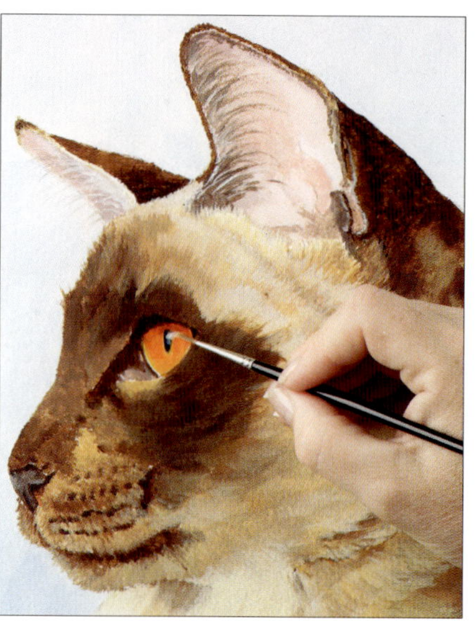 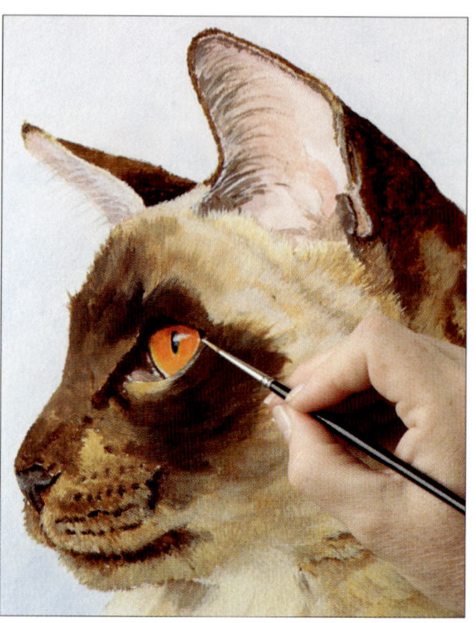

34 Return to your dark brown mix (burnt umber and French ultramarine) and further define the eye by adding it into the corner.

35 Darken the pupils with the pupil colour mix, making one side darker than the other, for where the shadows will catch it. Pick up some white and add in a white highlight on the eyeball by touching your brush to the pupil and dragging out a short stroke.

36 Using a pale caramel shade and one of the cream colours, add some highlights to the lower eyelid and around the eyeball.

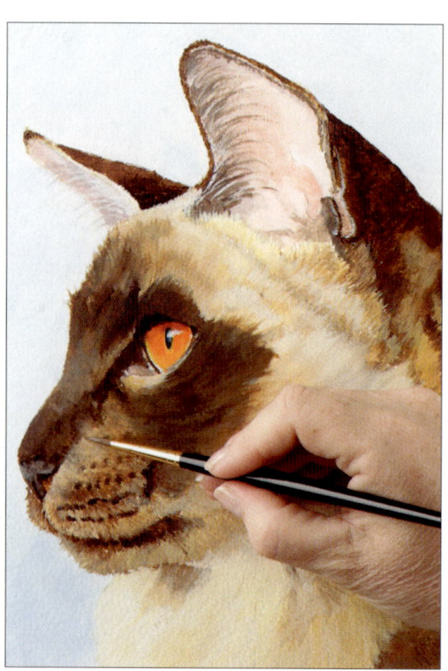 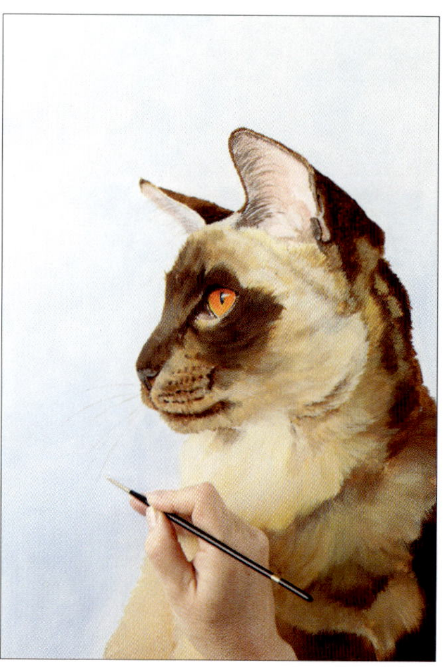 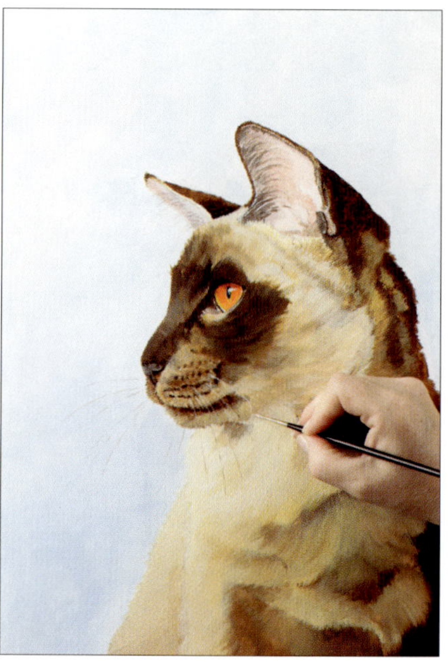

37 Add more depth and definition to the cat's nose area by stippling on the grey-brown mix, with a little burnt umber added in for the darker places. Use small, stippling strokes.

38 For the whiskers which will rest on the background, use a size 3 round brush with the grey-brown mix.

39 Make the grey-brown mix a bit lighter by adding in a touch more white, and paint in the whiskers on the opposite side of the face. Alternate between the base and the tip of the whiskers in the two grey-brown shades.

Opposite

The finished painting shown reduced in size.

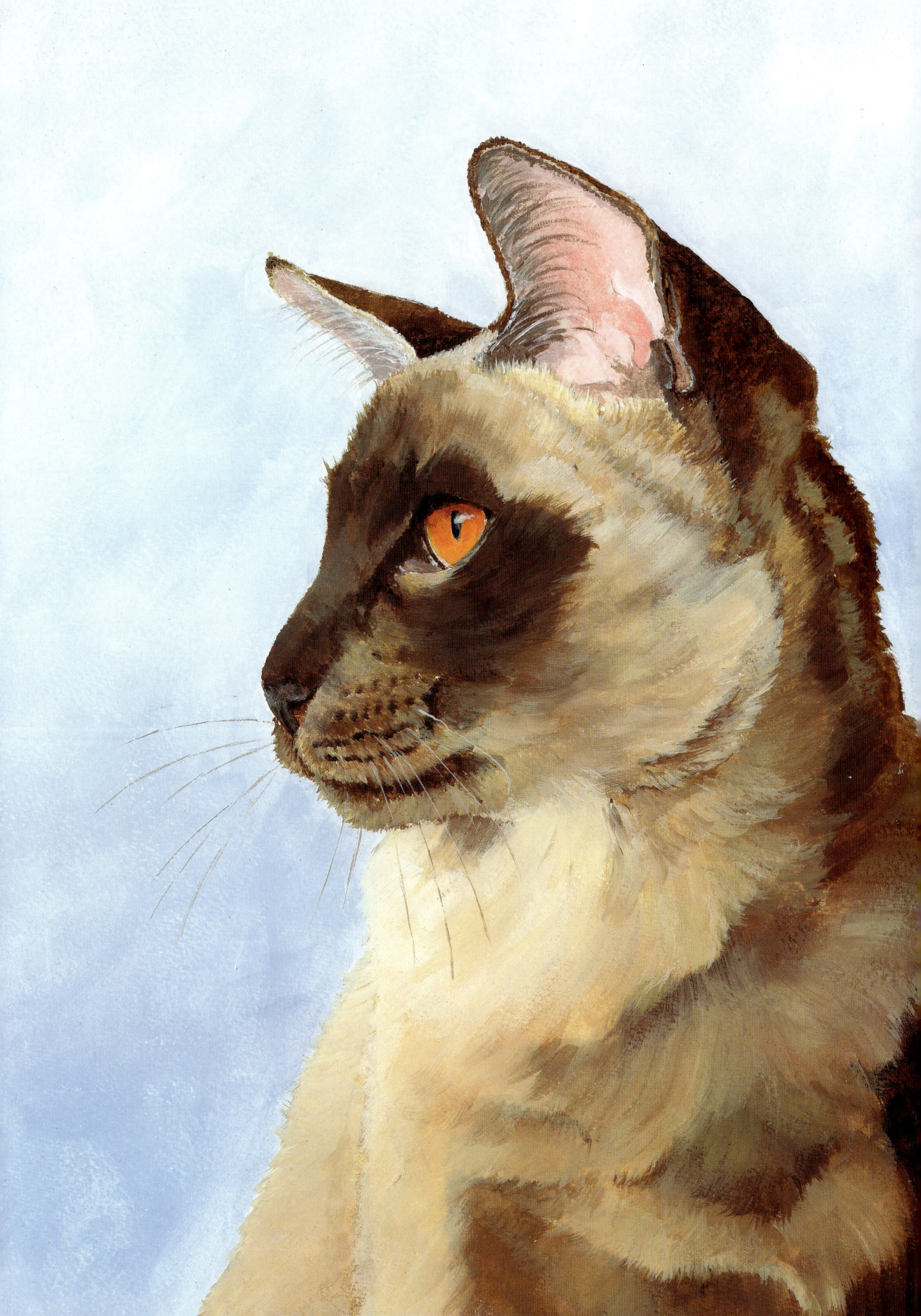

Festive Fun

When you are only a few weeks old, the whole world is new, and full of good stuff to play with. Here the softness of this fluffy kitten and the sparkly tinsel make a nice contrast of texture. We can have fun too, making use of loose expressive brushwork for the tinsel and softly blended shades for the fur.

Tip

To give depth to dark fur, start with an underpainting of lighter, warmer browns that will show through the dark layers.

You will need

300gsm (140lb) Rough or Not cold-pressed 100% watercolour paper

Colours: raw sienna, cadmium red, cadmium yellow, burnt sienna, French ultramarine, alizarin crimson, yellow ochre, burnt umber, titanium white, Prussian blue, cerulean blue, cobalt blue, Hooker's green

Brushes: size 1 round, size 2 round, size 3 round, size 4 round, 3mm (⅛in) flat, 5mm (³⁄₁₆in) flat, 6mm (¼in) flat, 10mm (⅜in) flat, size 6 filbert

Eraser

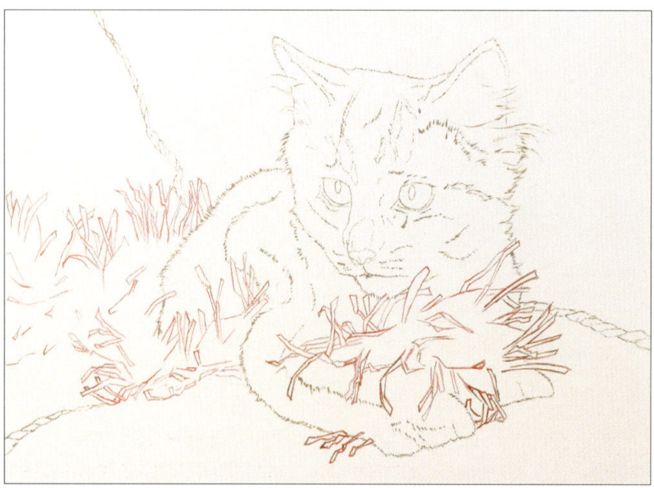

1 Transfer tracing 3 on to watercolour paper as shown on page 9. Outline the kitten with diluted raw sienna, and the tinsel in cadmium red using a size 1 or 3 round brush.

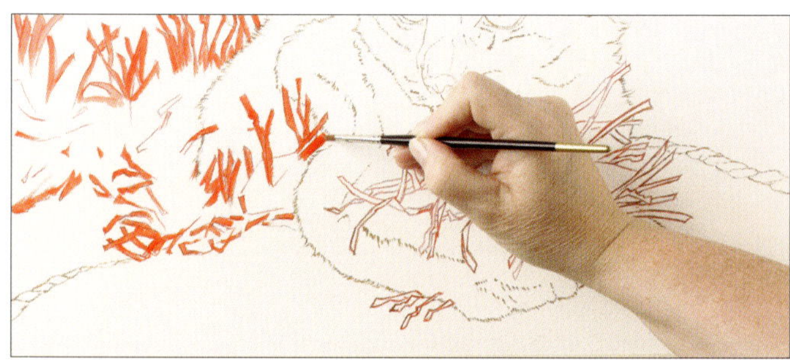

2 Change to a 3mm (⅛in) flat brush and, using cadmium red, start to block in the strands of tinsel on the outer edges.

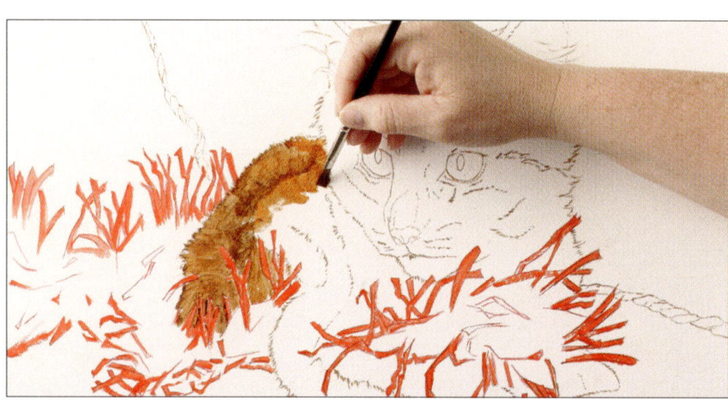

3 Underpaint the kitten with a mid-brown mix of burnt sienna and French ultramarine using the 6mm (¼in) flat brush. Change to a size 4 round to apply colour in between the tinsel strands. Alternate between this mix and make a slightly darker brown mix by adding more French ultramarine to it. Blend the two colours to create texture.

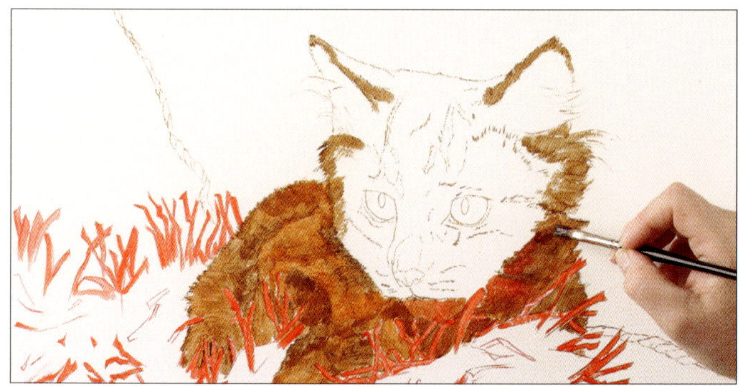

4 Prepare a reddish-brown mix using burnt sienna and alizarin crimson and apply to the chin and the right-hand side of the face – this will show as reflected light from the tinsel. Continue to work the rest of the edge of the face in the burnt sienna and French ultramarine mix.

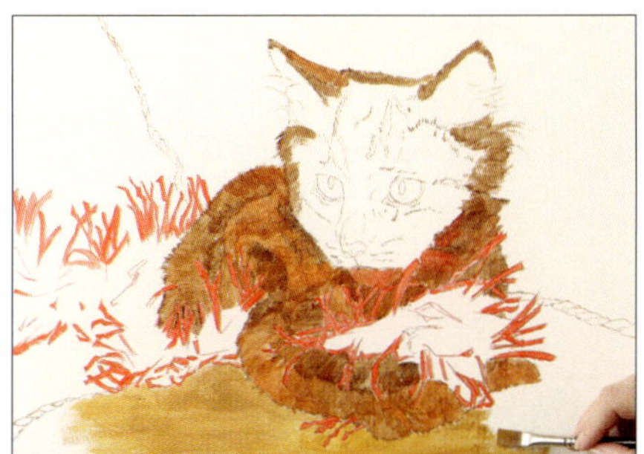 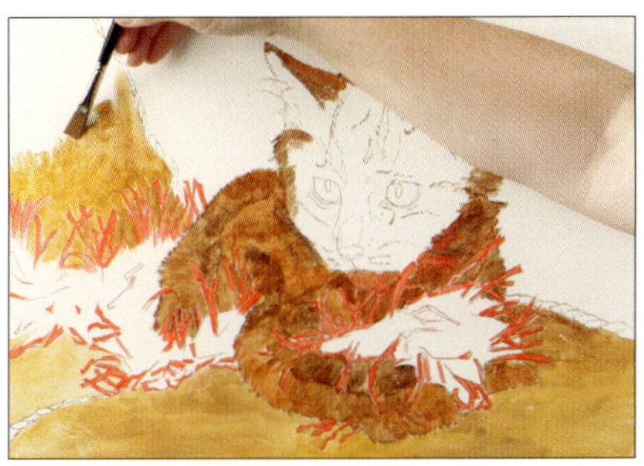 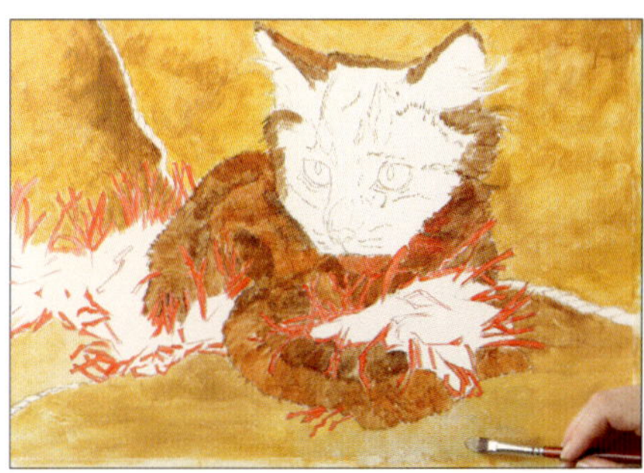

5 Prepare various caramel colours by adding yellow ochre to the mid-brown mix with varying amounts of white to produce a few different shades. Use these shades to block in the background cushions the kitten is sitting on, using the 10mm (⅜in) flat brush. Block in the rest of the background, avoiding the braiding.

6 Go in a little darker just behind the tinsel by adding a touch more mid-brown and blending with the caramel background. Continue with the background in this way.

7 Change to a size 6 filbert and using a light caramel mix, apply soft, stippling strokes. Add a few other caramel shades and a cream-coloured mix of cadmium yellow and white.

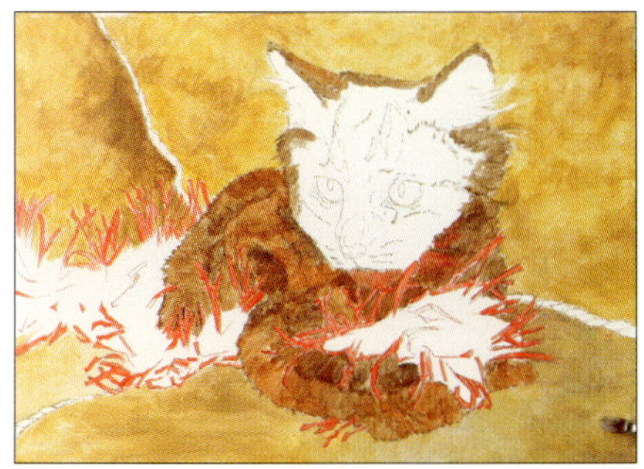 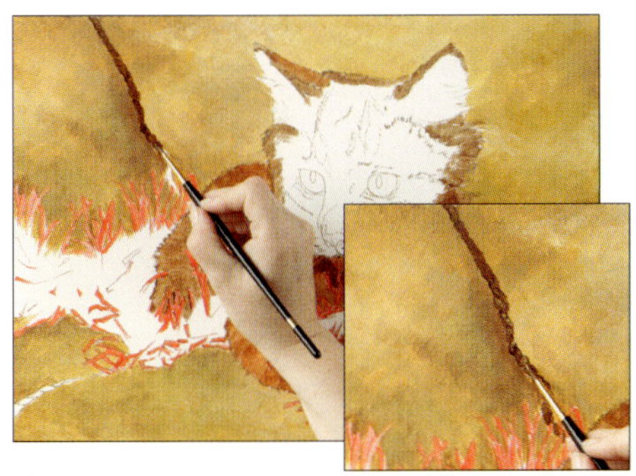 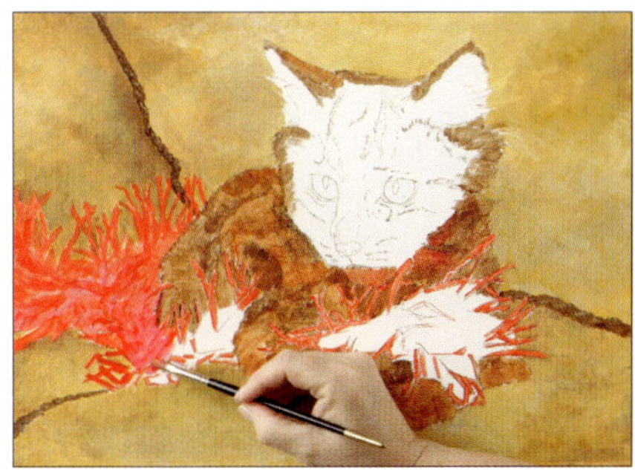

8 Work a little darker from the edges to keep the lightness around the kitten. This will help to make it the focal point. Darken the far left corner, and then go back over the area, lightening again and stippling and blending around the kitten.

9 Use burnt umber for the cushion cord and blend in a mid-caramel colour for texture. Describe the twist of the cord with some pale yellow ochre.

10 Using the 6mm (¼in) flat brush, block in the rest of the tinsel with the cadmium red. Add in a few flecks of alizarin crimson as you go, for interest. Don't be too rigid when painting the tinsel – work quite loose and free to give the impression of the tangled strands.

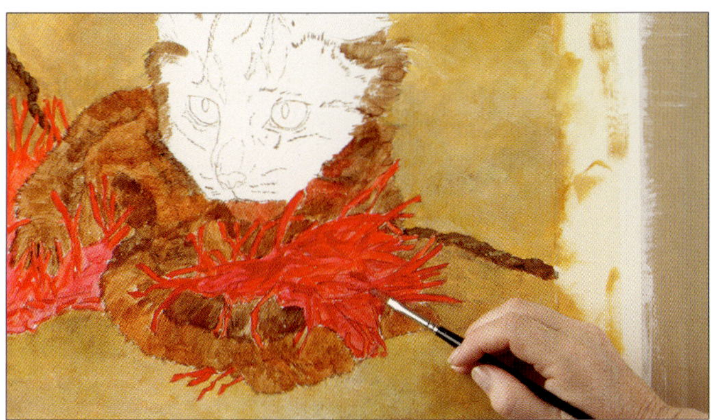 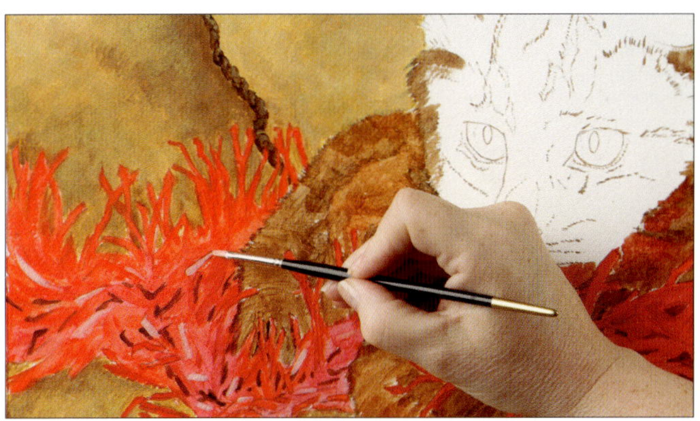

11 Change to the 3mm (⅛in) flat brush and, using a mix of burnt umber and cadmium red, pick out some dark points in the tinsel.

12 Prepare a pink mix using cadmium red and white and use it to add highlights on the tinsel strands, working from left to right. Using a darker strength of alizarin crimson, add in some dark brushstrokes to describe another colour of the tinsel strands. Try to produce various red tones for the tinsel. Leave to dry.

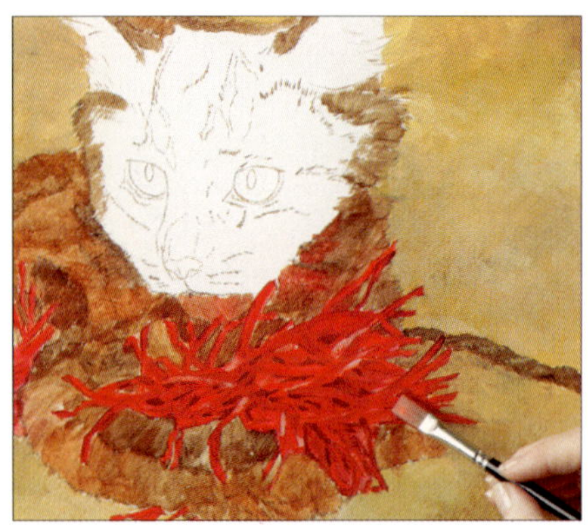

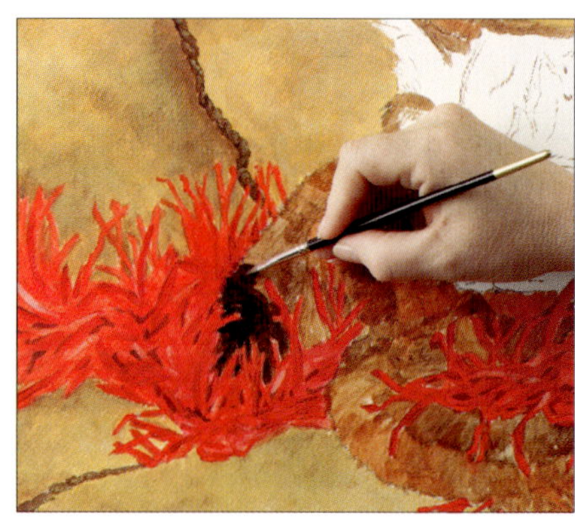

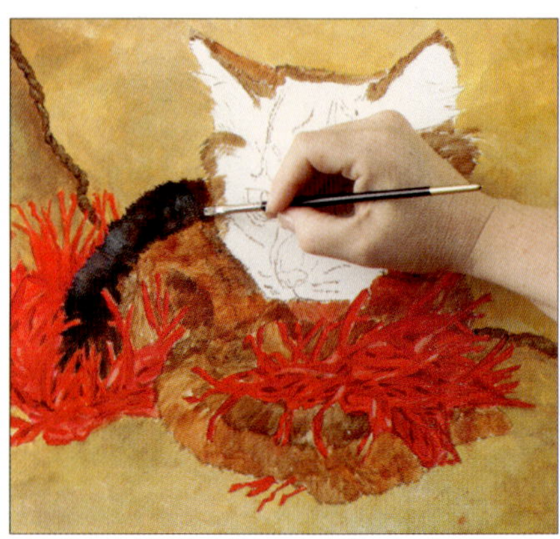

13 Using the 10mm (⅜in) flat brush, apply a thin glaze of cadmium red over the tinsel, thin enough for the other colours to show through. This will bring everything together, and make the tinsel look more solid. Use a thin glaze of alizarin crimson over the darker areas in the same way.

14 Change to a 5mm (³⁄₁₆in) flat brush and prepare two brown mixes: burnt umber and for a very dark brown, burnt umber with Prussian blue. Apply these shades to the lower back of the kitten, alternating and blending them.

15 Blend in a highlight of Prussian blue and white into the very dark brown, using on-off strokes with the flat of the brush to create fluffy fur. Work your way up the kitten's back, alternating between the two shades of brown (step 14) and adding highlights where the kitten's body catches the light. You might want to use a size 1 or 2 round brush to pull out some highlights to look like fur.

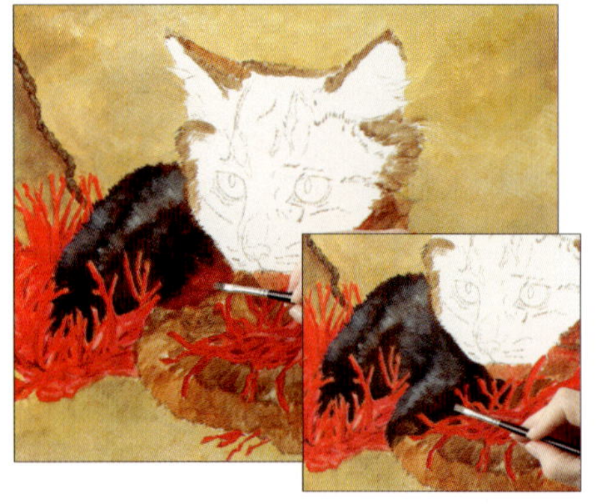

16 Apply a burnt sienna and alizarin crimson mix to the areas where the tinsel would reflect a reddish light on to the kitten's fur. Leave to dry slightly before painting the dark brown mixes over the top. Paint the darkest areas – under the chin and the top lip – using the very dark brown mix. You are not aiming for solid coverage but for brushstrokes that allow the previous colours to show through.

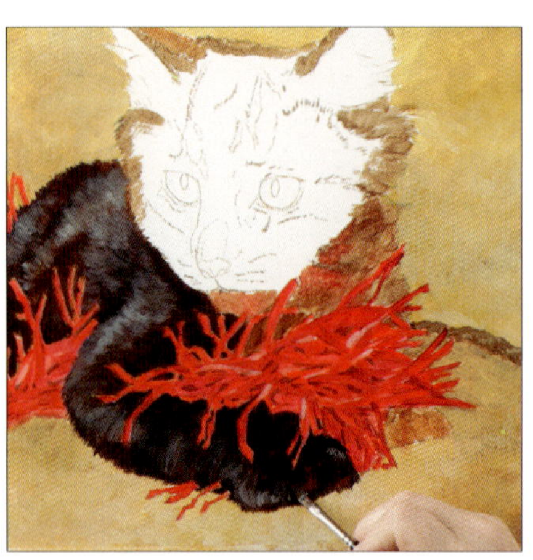

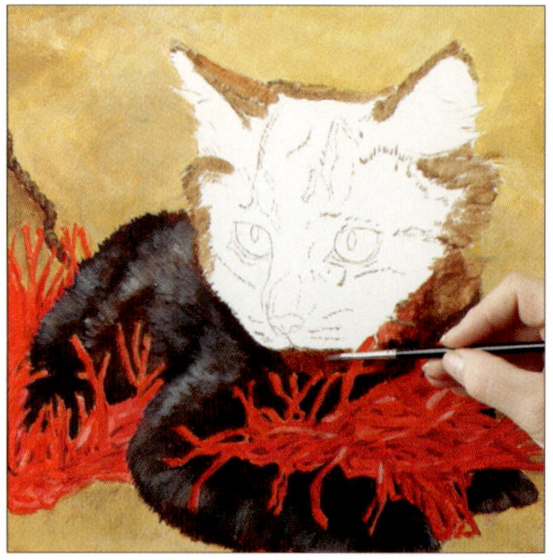

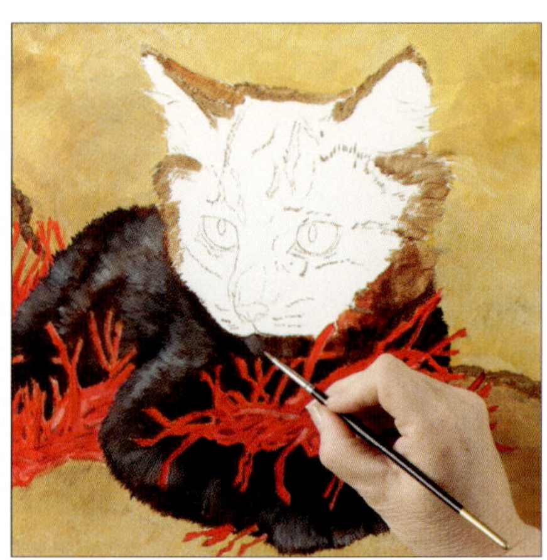

17 Add some brighter blue highlights using the highlight mix and add touches of the burnt sienna and alizarin crimson mix (step 16) to warm up the black fur. Work your way along the kitten's paws in the same way as for the back.

18 Change to a 3mm (⅛in) flat brush and prepare another reddish-brown mix: burnt umber and alizarin crimson. Paint on to the chin, working outwards from the lips using fairly short brushstrokes to allow the base colour to show through.

19 Repeat with the burnt umber. Add a touch of alizarin crimson to the highlight mix and add highlights to the chin.

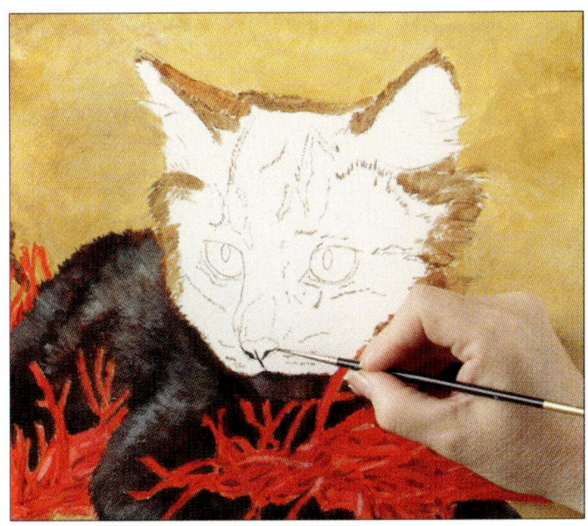

20 Add the very dark brown mix into the centre of the lip and pull out a few short strokes along the lipline using a size 1 round brush. Using the same mix, outline and define the side of the nose and the nostril and mark in the follicles of the kitten's whiskers on the muzzle.

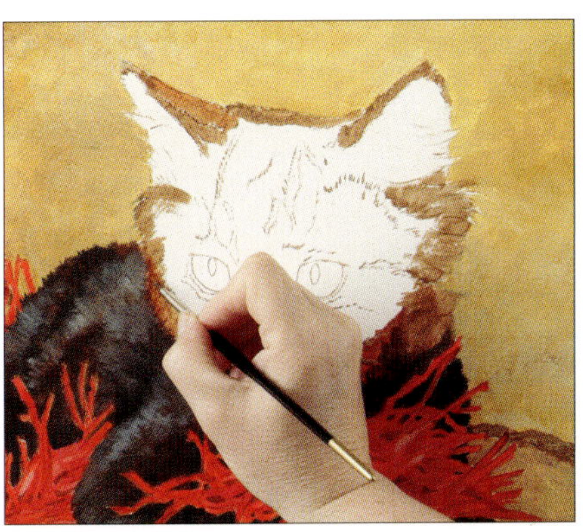

21 Apply the mid-brown mix (step 3) to the left-hand side of the kitten's face. It is easier and best practice to build up the face in sections to avoid losing vital detail.

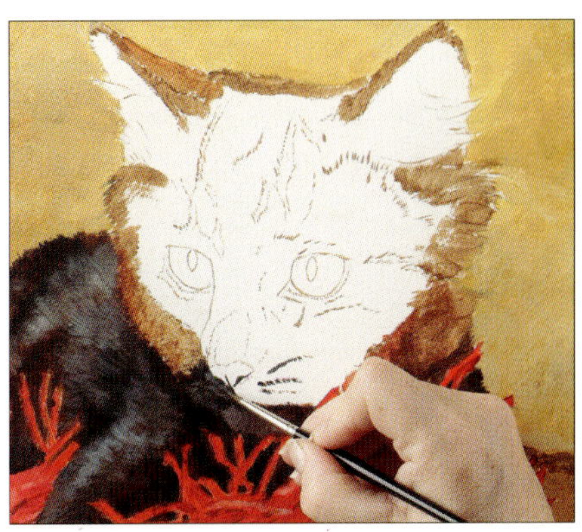

22 Add the burnt umber to the left-hand side of the lip, and pick out some highlights with the highlight mix. Using the same mix, and working from the outer edge of the lip, build up the brushstrokes to give the impression of a fluffy lip.

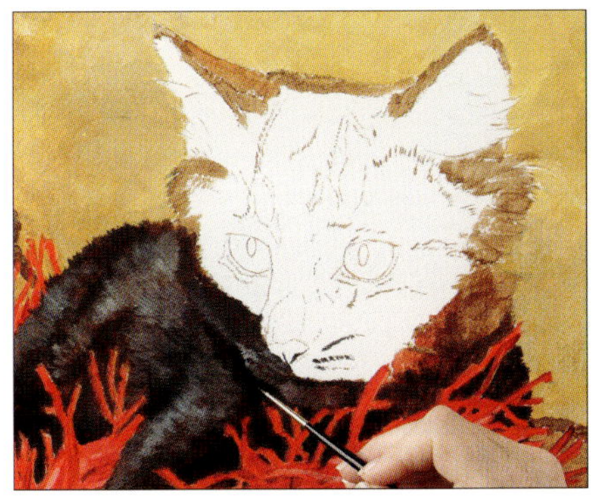

23 Apply the very dark brown mix from the cheek area down to the lip and apply the highlight mix to the edge of the face to prevent it blending into the kitten's body. Use a size 3 round brush to pull out some individual highlights and strengthen the shadow on the lips with the very dark brown mix.

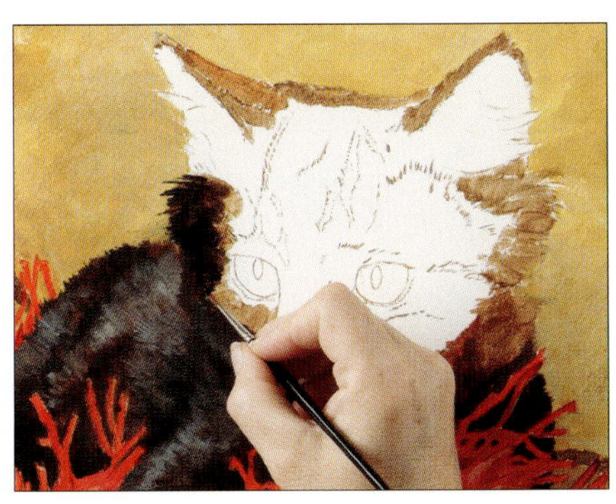

24 Using longer, curving brushstrokes, block in some more of the face with the very dark brown mix. Use smaller strokes around the bottom of the eye. Use the edge of the brush to pull out some thick tufts of fur above and to the left of the eye.

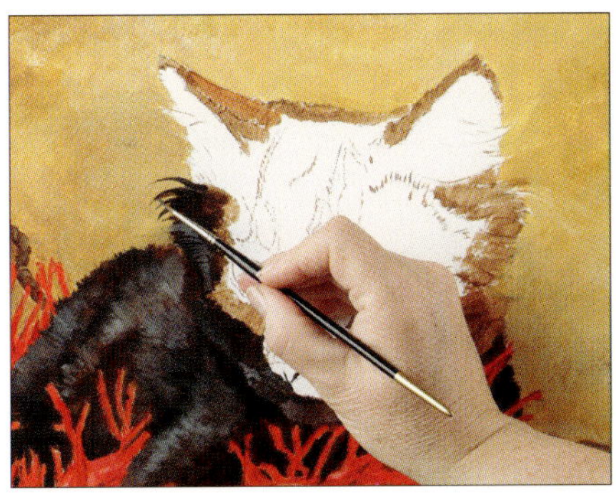

25 Continue to work these short strokes down the side of the face. Alternate between the very dark brown mix and burnt umber. Overlap these sections and pull out the colour to create a fluffy edge. Add some highlights to this area using the highlight mix. Use a size 2 round brush to pull out some individual strands of fur using the very dark brown mix.

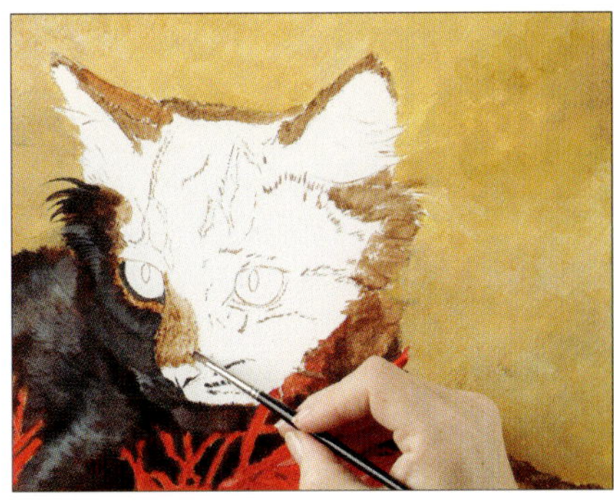

26 Move down and work up the cheek with the same mixes; add highlights and blend the varying shades. Outline the left eye with the very dark brown mix. Apply the mid-brown mix to the underneath of this eye, and then continue to block in this colour down the length of the nose.

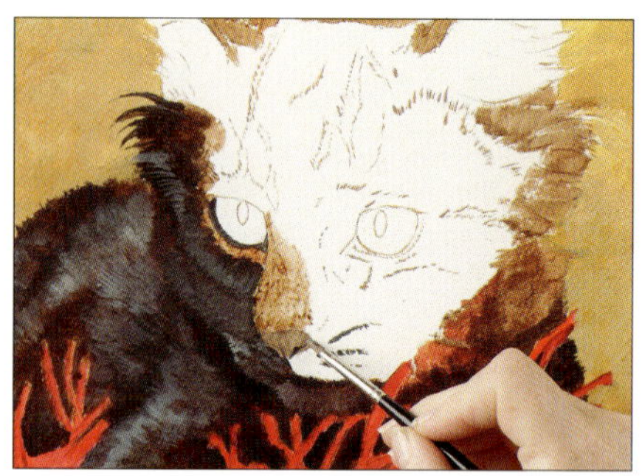

27 Prepare a beige colour for the nose by adding a little of the highlight colour to burnt umber. Apply this mix to the tip of the nose.

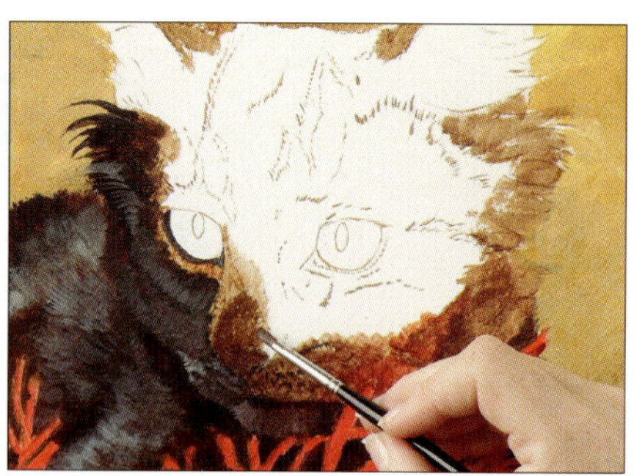

28 Apply the mid-brown mix to the right side of the lip and add in the reddish-brown mix (step 4). Use the beige mix for highlights on the area on the top of the nose. Stipple this colour on.

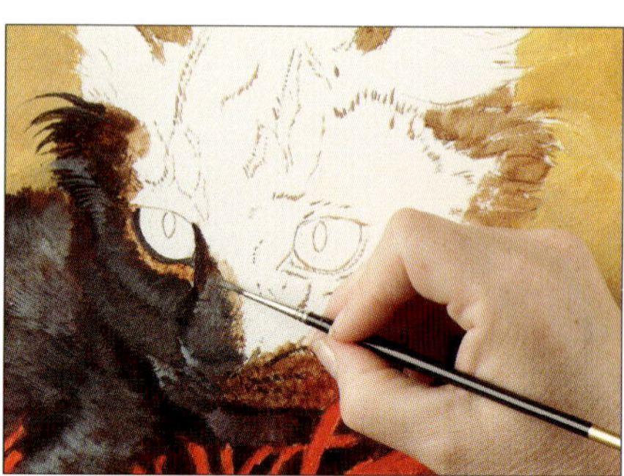

29 Stipple the two colours either side of the dark line so you get a soft edge, and define the left edge of the nose with the highlight mix. Add the very dark brown to the side of the nose and blend with the highlight colour. Work this colour up from the nose into the corner of the eye.

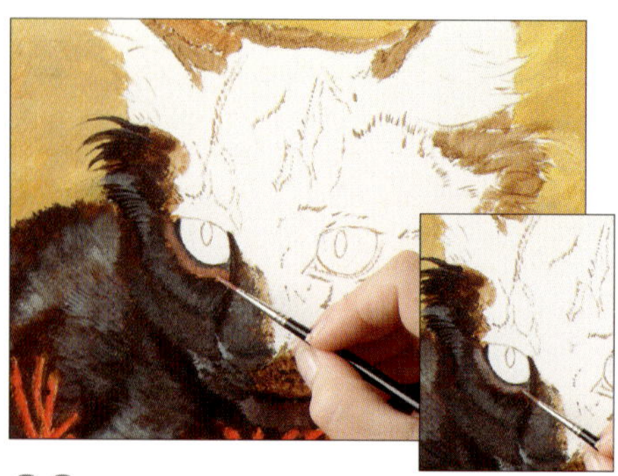

30 Add some cobalt blue to your pink mix to make a lilac-pink colour, and apply it just under the eye on to the mid-brown layer. Pick up some burnt umber to refine the eye shape.

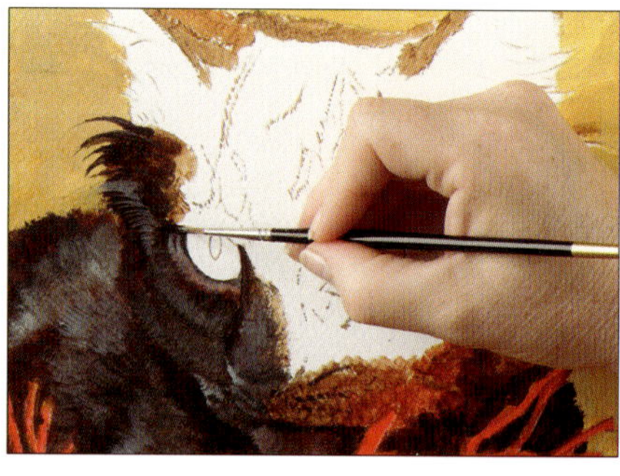

31 Pick up the highlight colour and blend and feather away from the dark outline of the eye. Feather out from the top corner of the eye. Add the very dark brown to this top corner to cut through the highlight colour and add shadow.

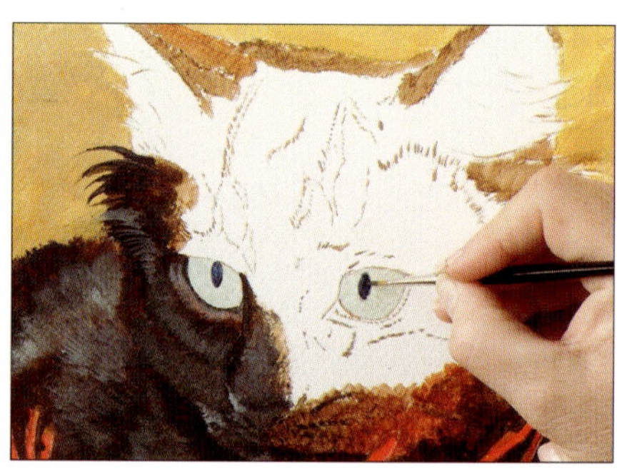

32 To work on the eyes, prepare a base colour of pale green: cadmium yellow, cerulean blue and white, and block them in using a 3mm (⅛in) flat brush. Change to a size 1 round brush and paint in the pupils using a mix of Hooker's green and French ultramarine.

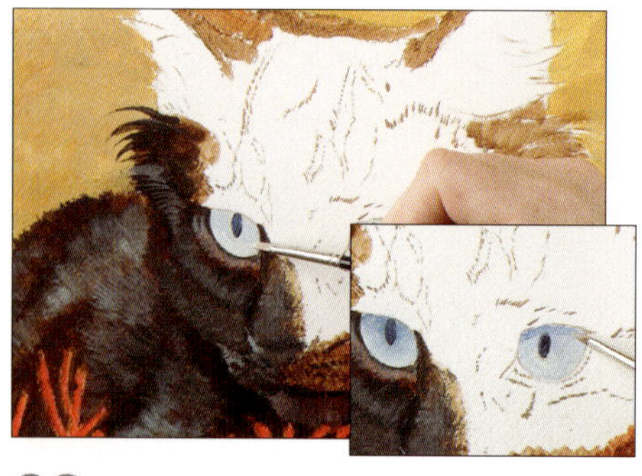

33 Apply a mix of cobalt blue and white over the base colour of the eyes, blending to a paler mix towards the bottom of each eye. Add a touch of Hooker's green to this mix and apply to the top of each eye and feather.

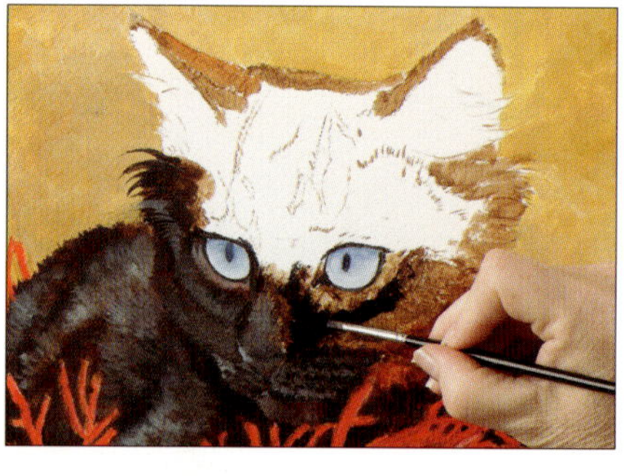

34 Outline the right-hand eye with the very dark brown mix using the size 1 round. Change to a 3mm (⅛in) flat brush and build up the kitten's face using the same colour mixes and techniques as used for the left side of the face.

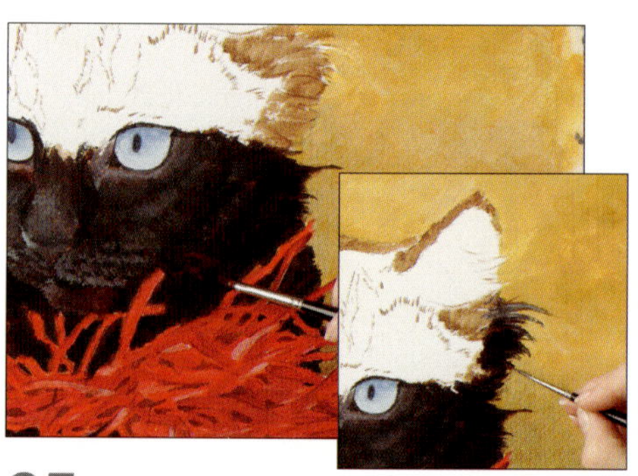

35 Add some alizarin crimson to the highlight colour in places, for example around the right lip and mouth. Add in a few strands of hair to the right-hand side of the head using the same technique as for the left-hand side.

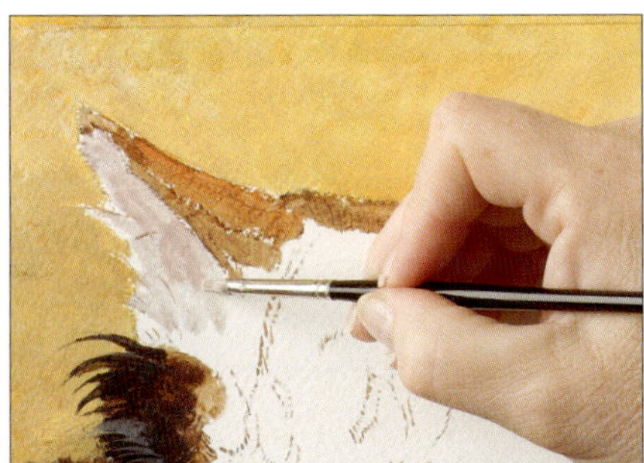

36 Add the pink-lilac mix to the inside of the ears. Apply a more lilac shade to the edges and a pinker shade towards the centre of the ears.

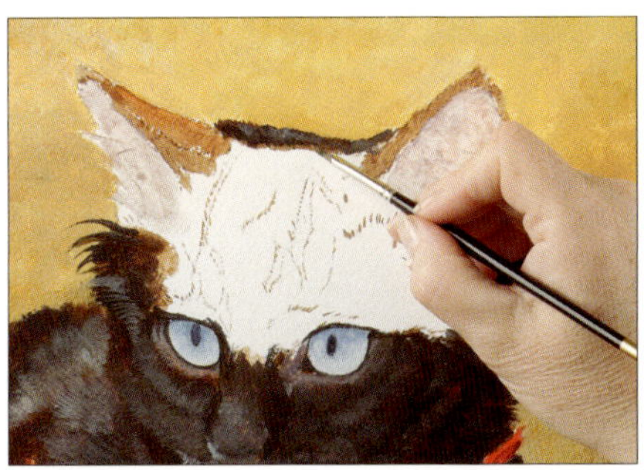

37 Work up the top of the kitten's head using the same colour mixes and techniques as for the rest of the face.

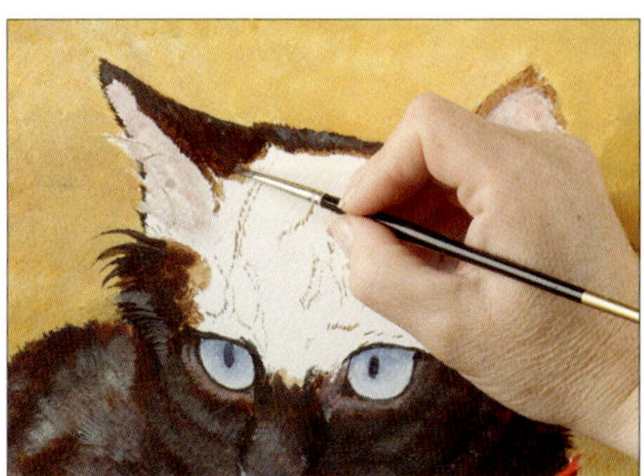

38 Outline the far edge of the ear in burnt umber and then work up the ears using the different face colour mixes.

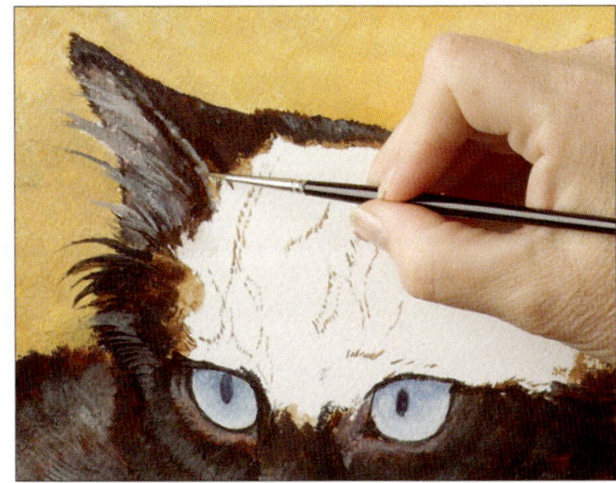

39 Add a grey colour (burnt umber, cobalt blue and white) with a touch of alizarin crimson, to the inside top of each ear. Using a size 1 round brush, build up the feathery tufts of fluff on the ears using different shades of the grey mix; some more grey-blue, some grey-lilac and so on.

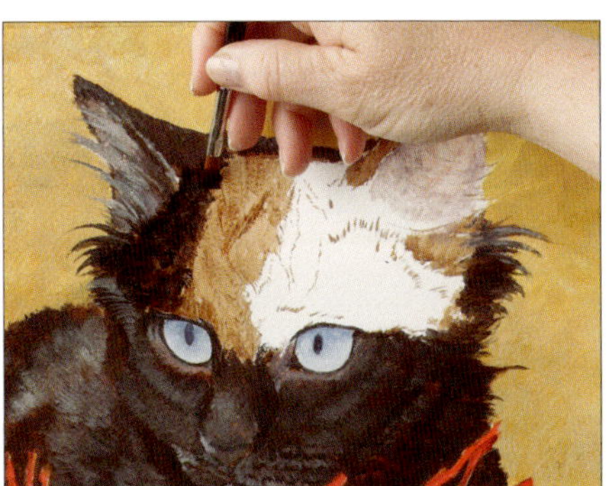

40 Working from left to right, work up the kitten's face, as before, starting with the base colour, the brown shades and finally adding in the highlights and blending.

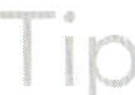

Tip

If you find that, when you are applying the highlights to the dark fur, the colours are blending too much, leave to dry slightly before applying the highlight on top, as another layer.

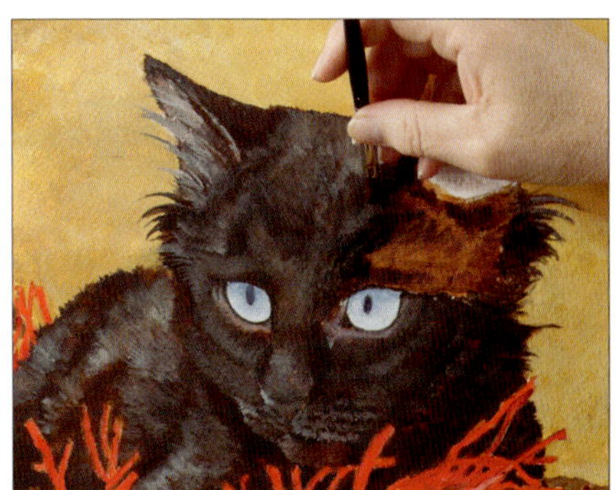

41 Add in the highlights and blend.

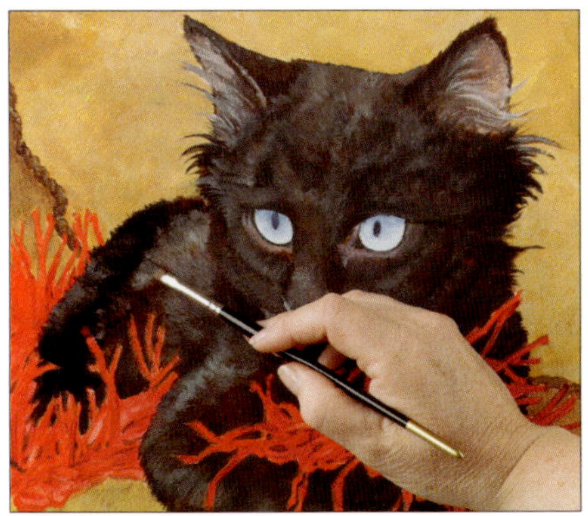

42 Prepare a thin mix of the very dark brown and apply this as a glaze over the kitten's body. This will soften the overall painting by taking down the sharpness of some of the highlights.

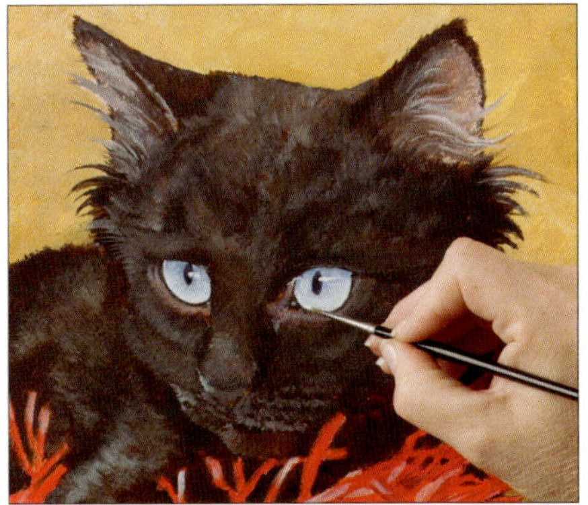

43 Using the same pupil colour mix, go back over the pupils to strengthen them using the size 1 round brush. Use white to mark on the highlights in the eyes.

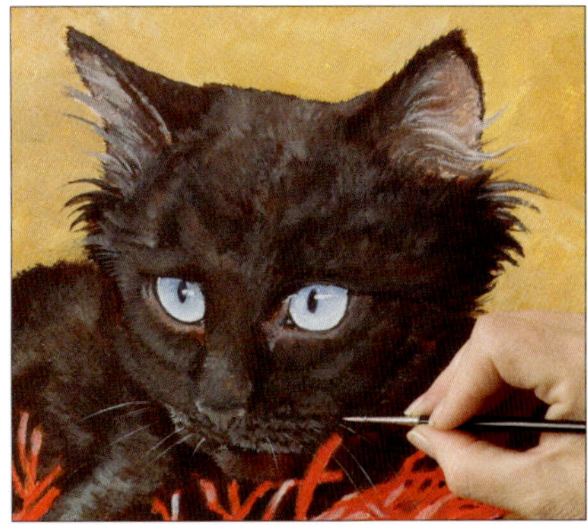

44 Finally, paint in the whiskers using the size 1 round brush and white with the grey mixes added.

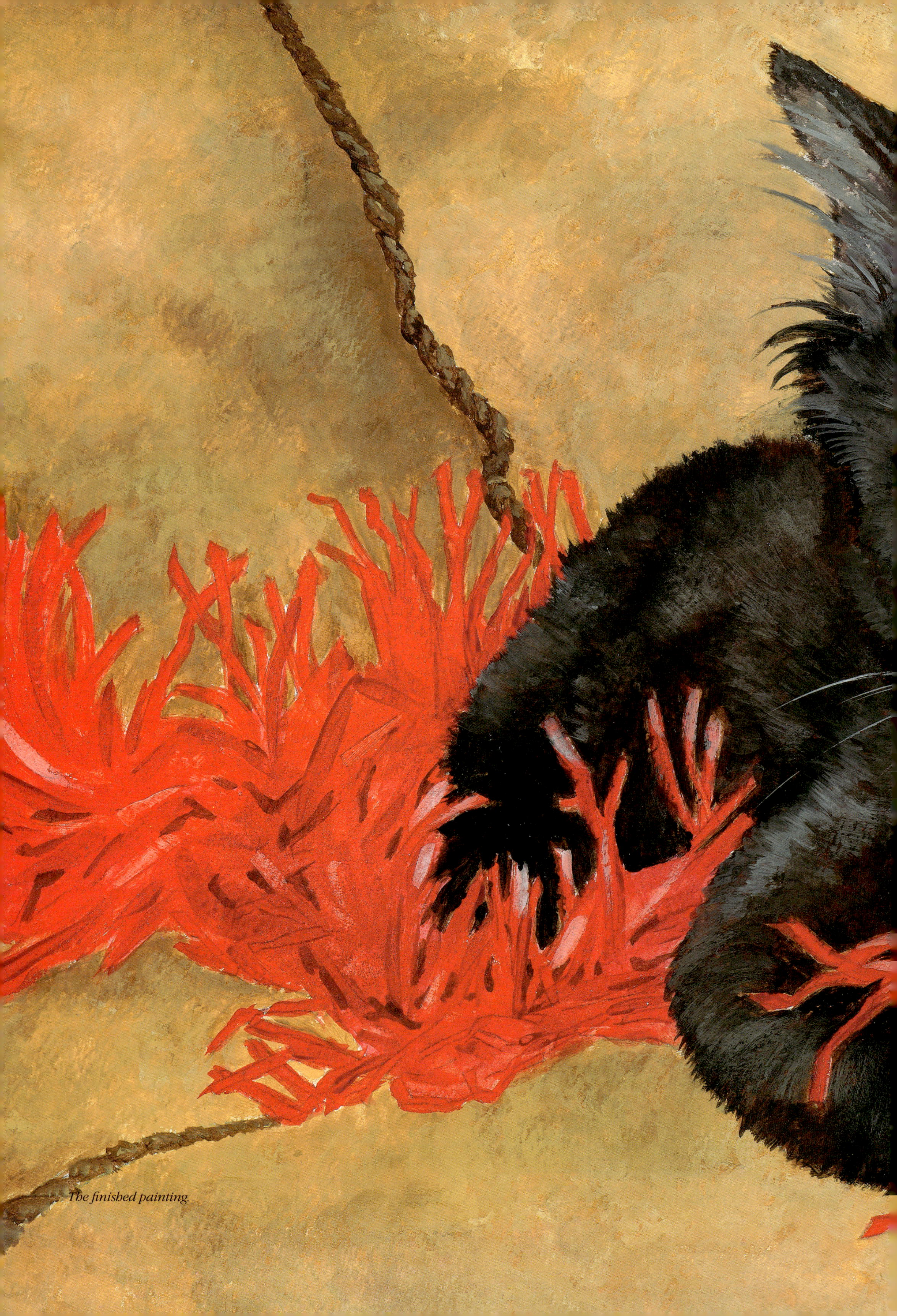

The finished painting.

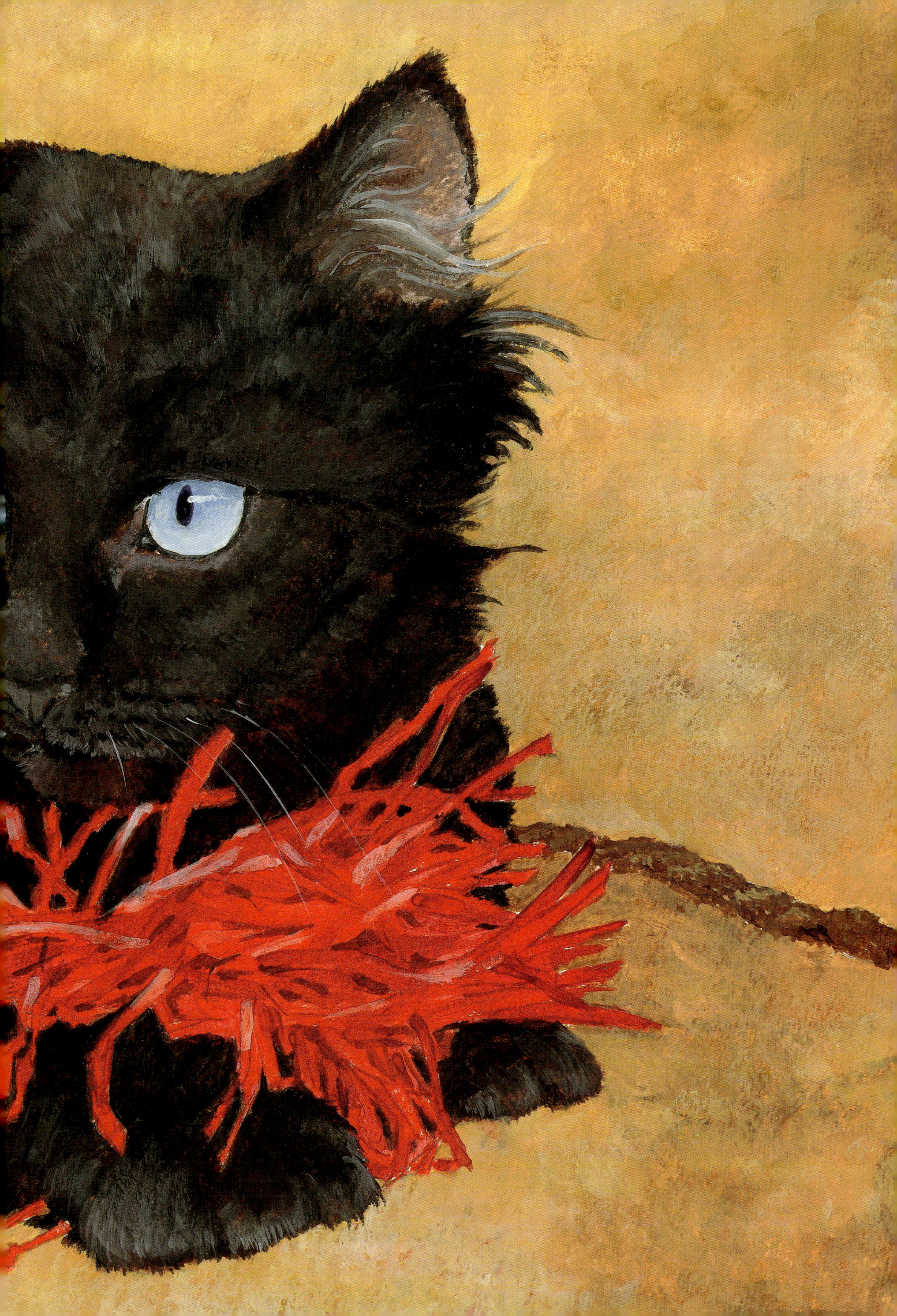

Double Trouble

Sharing your home with a pair of kittens is guaranteed to keep you smiling, as you never quite know what they will get up to next. They change tack in an instant, one moment they are asleep and the next they are chasing each other, a piece of string or a ball. Momentarily distracted by the camera, the little kitten on the right has taken his eye off the ball. Will his brother whisk it away from him?

Tip

If you would like to add more colour to this picture and make it your own, experiment with painting the floor tiles in different colours and vary the shades.

You will need

300gsm (140lb) Rough or Not watercolour paper

Colours: yellow ochre, titanium white, cobalt blue, burnt sienna, raw sienna, French ultramarine, alizarin crimson, Prussian blue, burnt umber, cadmium yellow, cadmium red, Hooker's green,

Brushes: size 1 round, size 2 round, size 3 round, size 6 filbert, 3mm (⅛in) flat, 5mm (³⁄₁₆in) flat, 15mm (⅝in) flat

Eraser

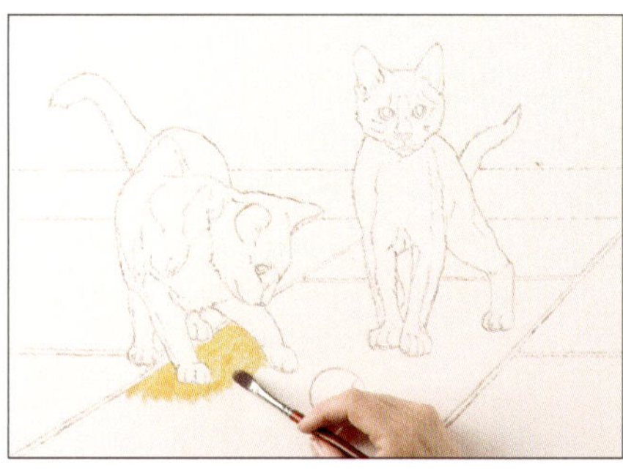

1 Transfer tracing 4 on to watercolour paper as shown on page 9. Outline the drawing with diluted raw sienna using a size 1 or 3 round brush.

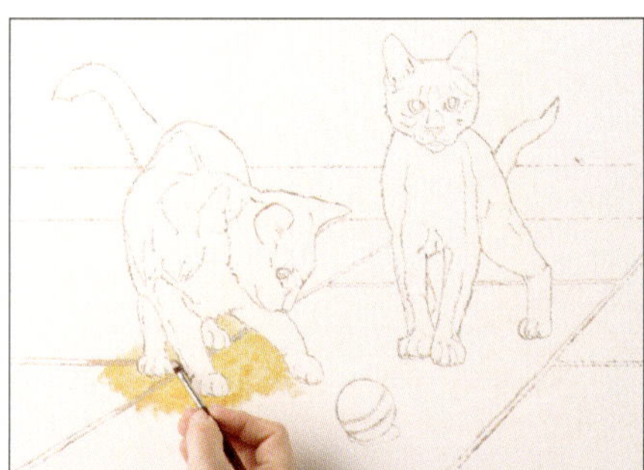

2 Using a size 6 filbert, block in the floor with a mix of yellow ochre and white to make a creamy yellow.

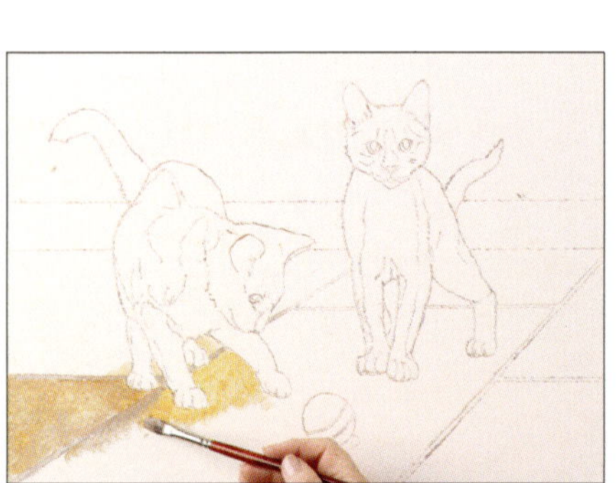

3 Prepare a mix of cobalt blue, white and burnt sienna to make a grey-beige. Use this mix to block in the gaps between the paving slabs on the floor. You do not need to produce very crisp, neat edges here – leave it looking rustic.

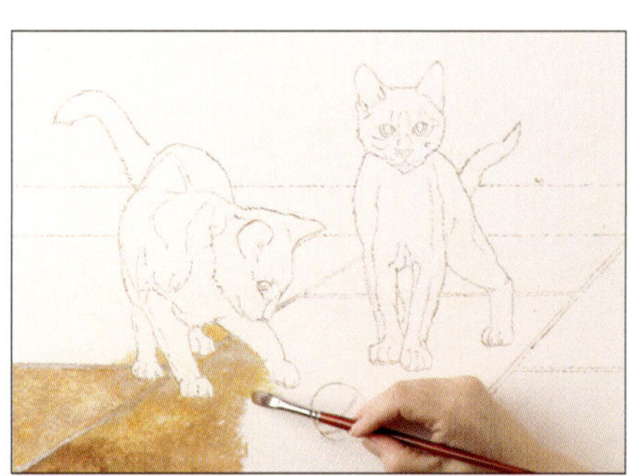

4 Stipple the grey-beige colour on top of the creamy yellow base to add texture. Make sure that no one colour is dominating to produce a subdued terracotta colour.

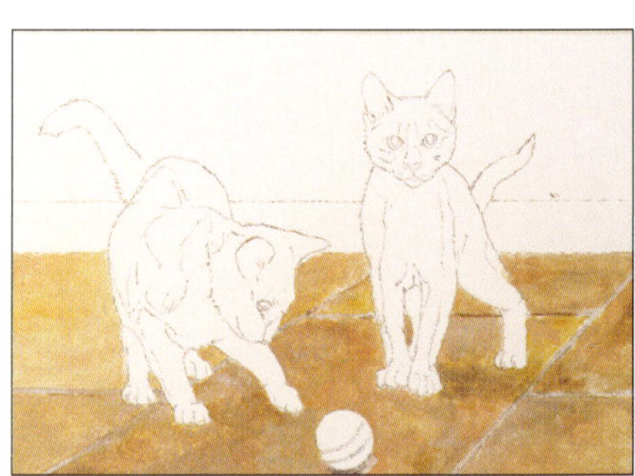

5 Continue to stipple in various caramel shades by varying the proportions of paint in your colour mixes. Start with the warmer shades and add the pale ones over the top.

6 Although you are working in different shades, be sure to carry some key colours between the slabs that are next to each other. This makes it look consistent.

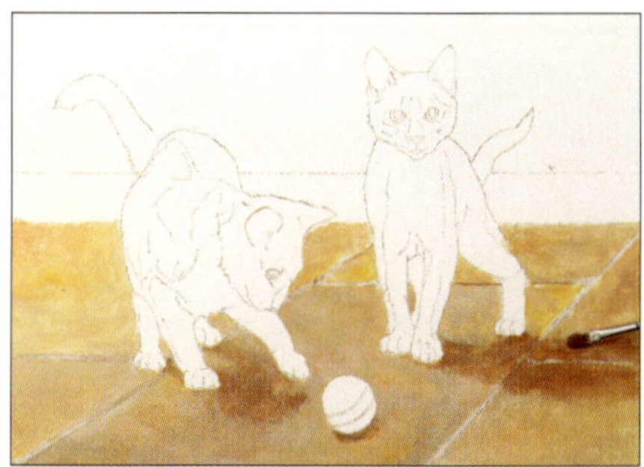

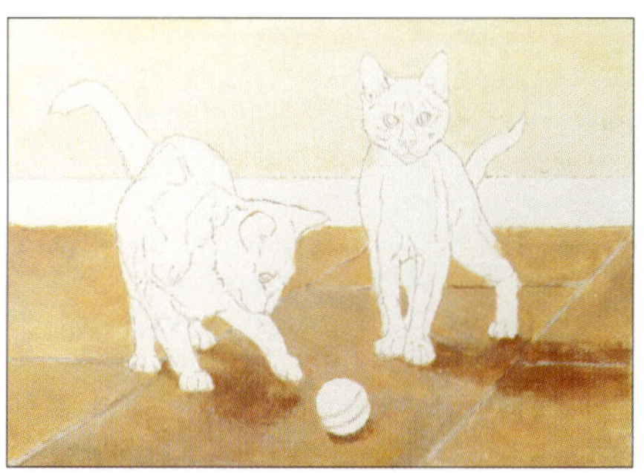

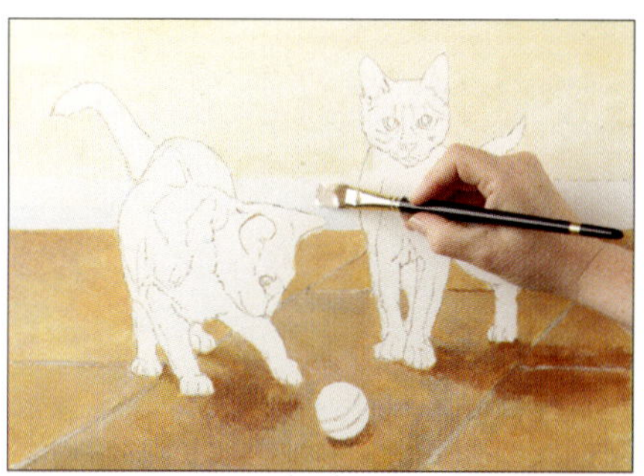

7 Use a mid-caramel tone for the shadows on the floor.

8 Change to a 15mm (⅝in) flat brush and block in the wall in the background using the creamy yellow mix.

9 Prepare a pale blue mix using white with a touch of cobalt blue, and block in the skirting board. Add slightly more blue to the bottom half of the skirting board to add some depth to the background. Use the full width of the brush, flat-on.

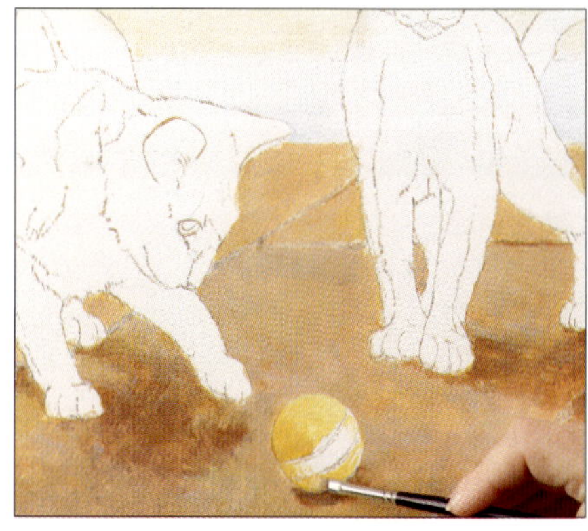

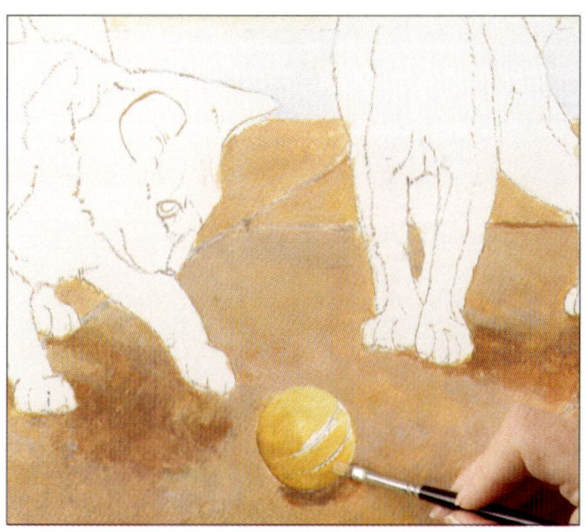

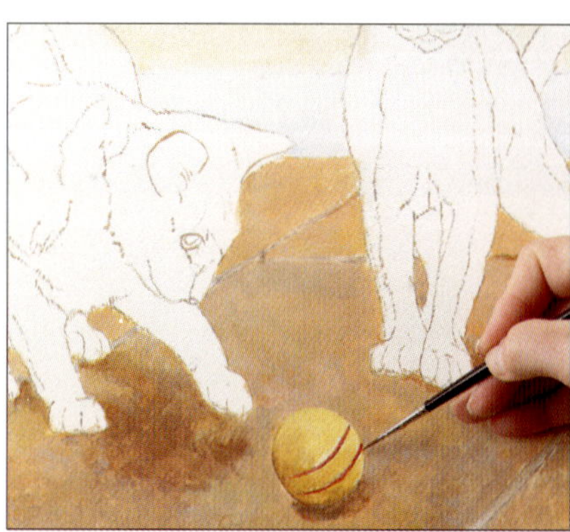

10 Change to a 5mm (³⁄₁₆in) flat brush for the ball and paint it using the creamy yellow mix. Prepare a lighter creamy-yellow mix from cadmium yellow and white and paint the top and right-hand side of the ball.

11 Add some of the darker caramel colours (from the floor mixes) for shadow and to add form to the far left-hand side and the underside, and work a little up the right-hand side of the ball.

12 Change to a size 1 round brush and, using alizarin crimson, paint the two red stripes on to the ball.

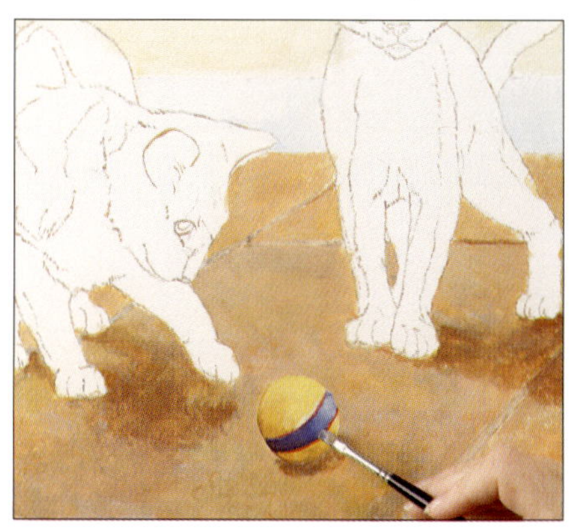

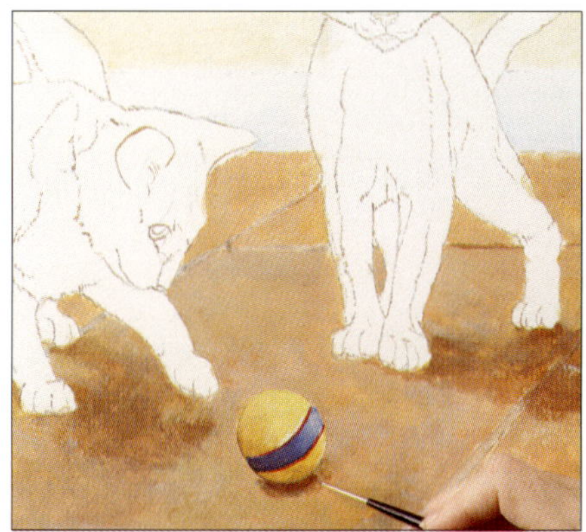

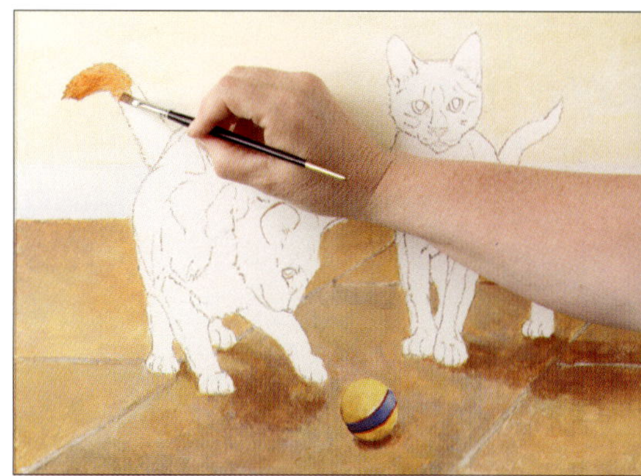

13 Return to the pale blue mix (step 9) and apply this between the two thin red stripes. Pull the colour down and blend with French ultramarine at the base of the ball. Add in a pure white highlight to the far right of the blue stripe.

14 Strengthen the shadows on and around the ball using the various caramel shades used for the floor.

15 Return to the 5mm (³⁄₁₆in) flat brush and apply a base wash of burnt sienna to the left-hand cat, starting from the tip of the tail.

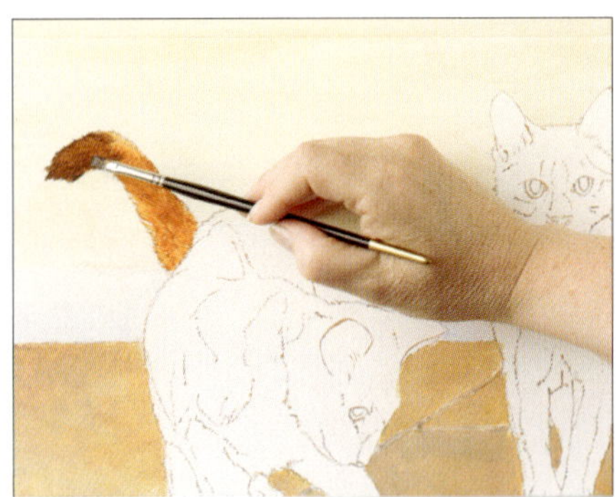

16 Prepare a brown mix using burnt umber and French ultramarine, and paint this over the burnt sienna base from the tip of the left-hand cat's tail.

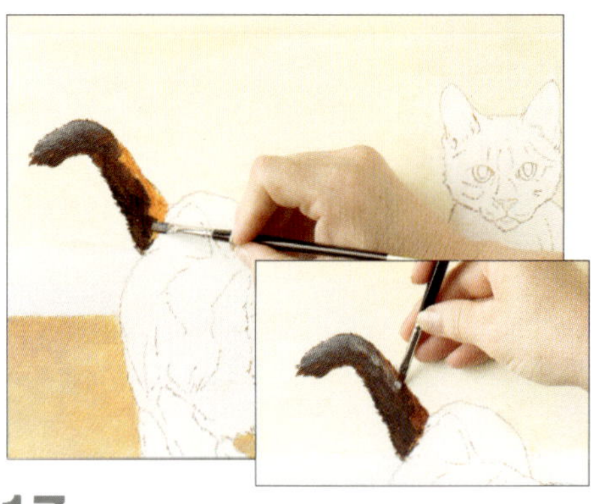

17 Prepare a dark brown mix of Prussian blue and burnt umber and apply this to the tail. Change to a size 3 round brush and pull out some paint from the tail to look like strands of hair. Add some highlights using a pale blue mix using white and Prussian blue.

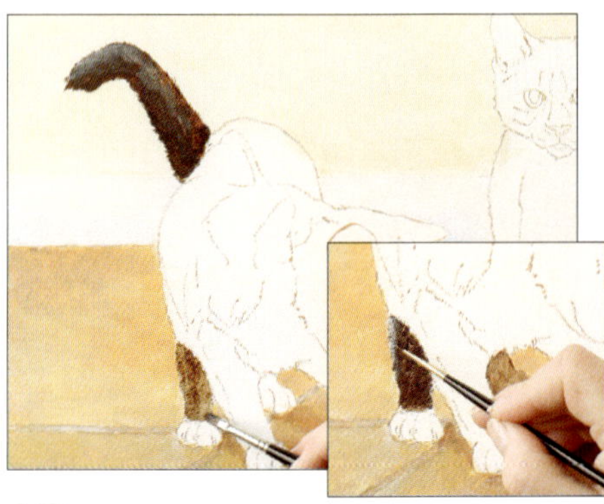

18 Apply the brown mix (step 16) to the left-hand cat's two back legs. Use the dark brown mix to add shadow to the legs, and the pale blue mix to add highlights.

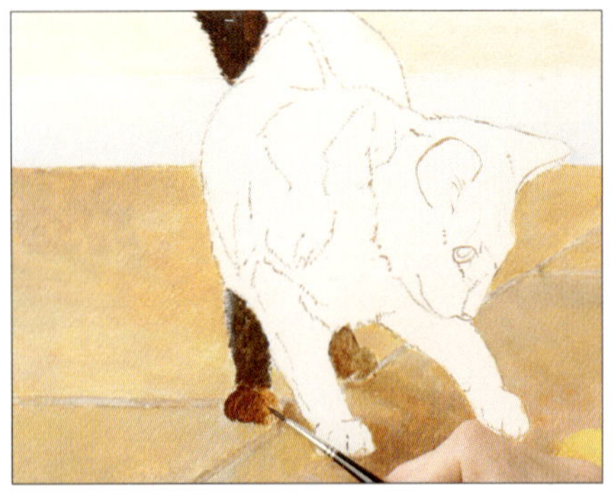

19 Change to a size 2 round brush and use burnt umber for the nearest paw on the back leg.

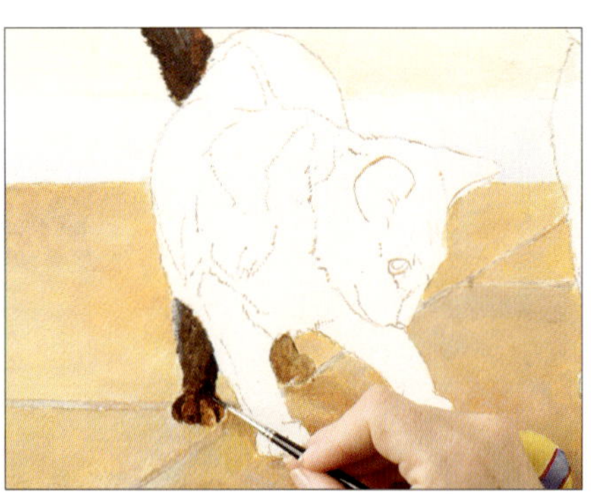

20 Add in the shadows using the dark brown mix to suggest the toes.

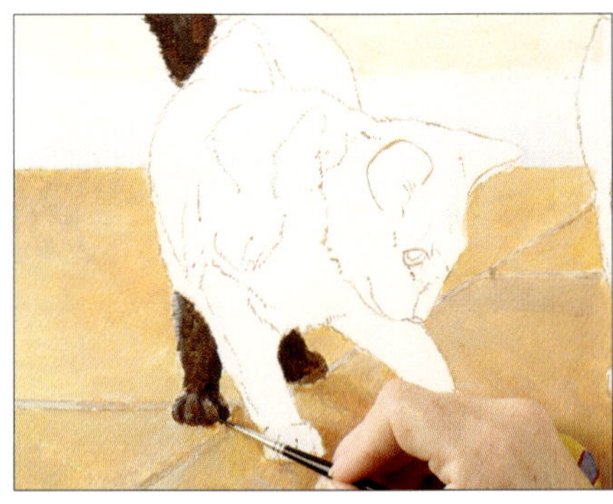

21 Add highlights to the back paws with the pale blue mix used in step 17.

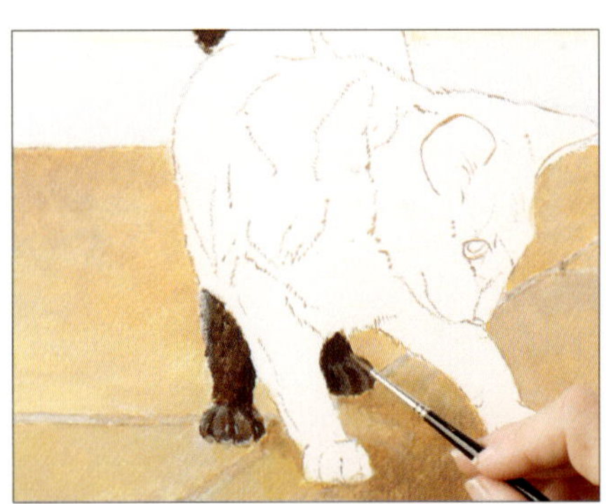

22 Using the grey-beige mix, paint in the paw pads and the claws. Blend the grey-beige with the burnt umber for a natural look and to add form to the paws and toes.

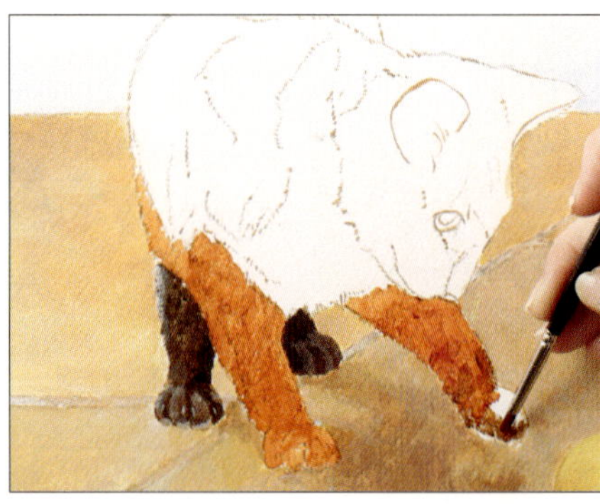

23 Change to a 3mm (⅛in) flat brush and block in the body and front legs with burnt sienna. Apply the brown mix to the paws to add shadow and form.

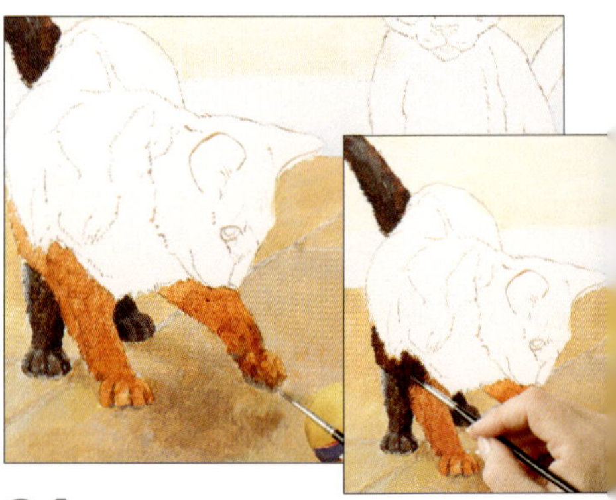

24 Run the grey-beige mix along the bottom of the paws on the front legs to describe the paw pads and paint in the claws using the same colour. Using the dark brown mix, work up the cat's body and front legs in sections.

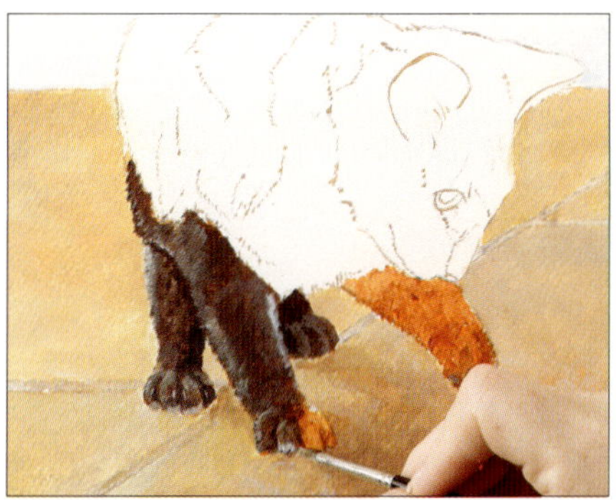

25 Add highlights using the pale blue mix (step 17) and blend with the dark brown. Continue to work in this way for the whole of the cat's body.

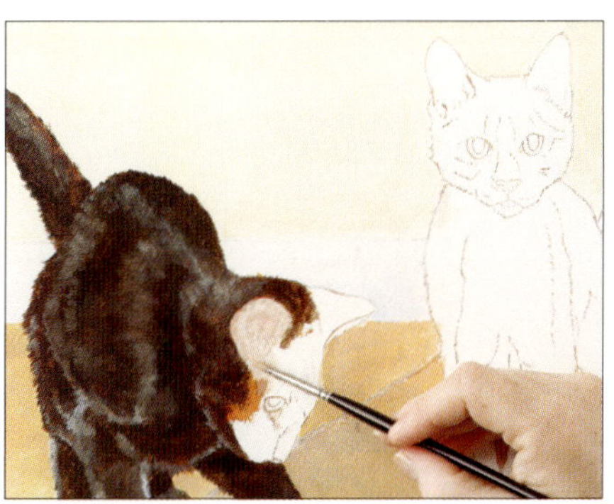

26 Change to a 3mm (⅛in) flat brush for the face and a size 1 round for the detail. Prepare a pink-lilac mix using white, cadmium red, cadmium yellow and cobalt blue and paint the inside of both cats' ears, and a touch on to each mouth. For the cat on the left, take the colour down towards the cat's eyes.

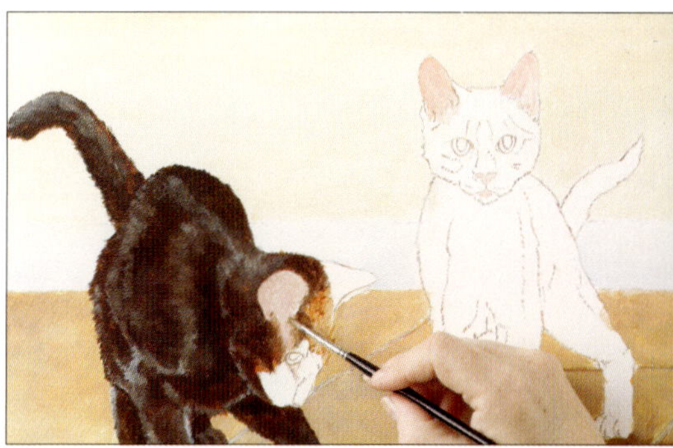

27 Feather in some burnt umber to the edges of this pink-lilac strip. Add some of the grey-beige mix to the insides of the ears for depth and shadow. Work up the rest of the left-hand cat's head and ears, in the same way as for the body.

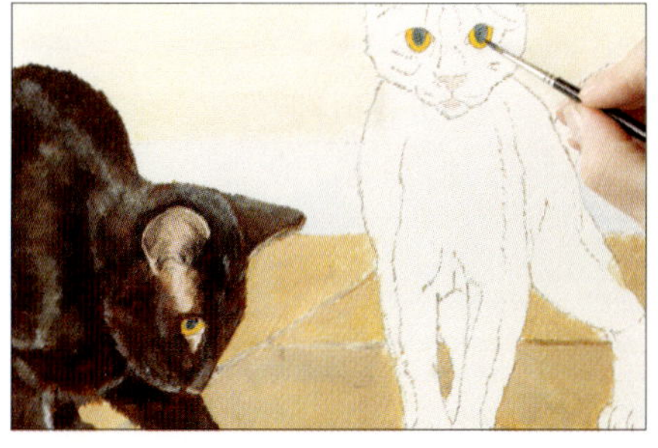

28 Change to a size 2 round brush and paint the irises using a mix of cadmium yellow and cadmium red. Paint the pupils using a mix of Hooker's green and French ultramarine. Repeat for the right-hand cat.

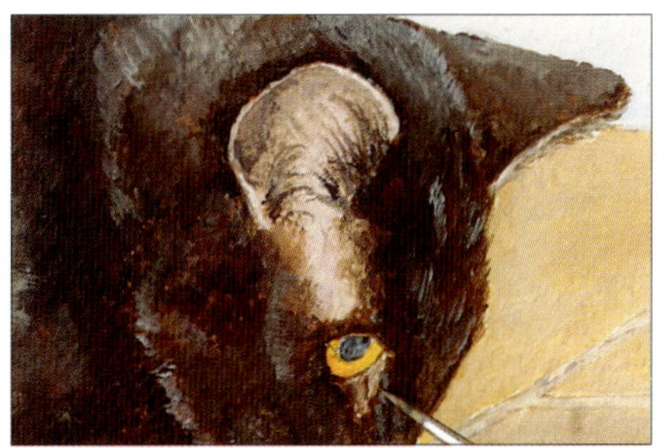

29 Add a touch of burnt umber to the pink-lilac mix and apply this to the inner corner of the left-hand cat's eye. Change to a size 3 round brush and using the dark brown mix, add in some shadow just under the eye. Pick up one of the pale blue mixes and add a few highlights around the eye.

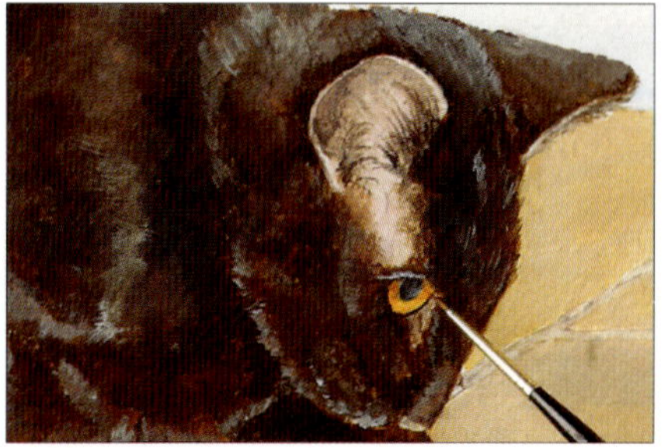

30 Return to the pupil colour and go back over the eyes to strengthen the colour; the pupil should be darkest at the top. Add a touch of burnt sienna to the iris colour and go back over this area, to strengthen the colour intensity. Apply the darkest shades at the top of the irises for shadow.

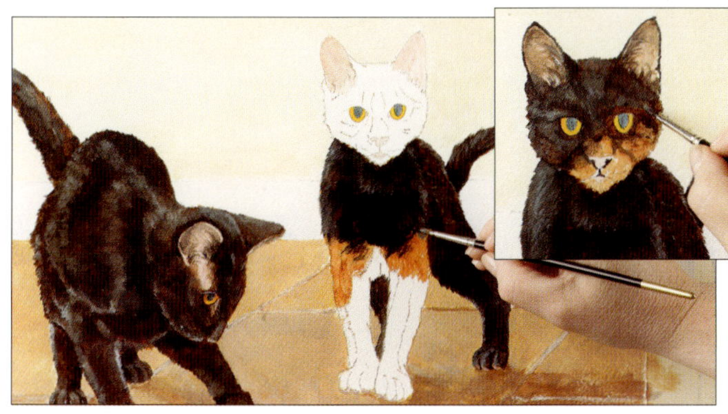

31 Work up the other cat's fur on the body and head in the same way as for the left-hand cat.

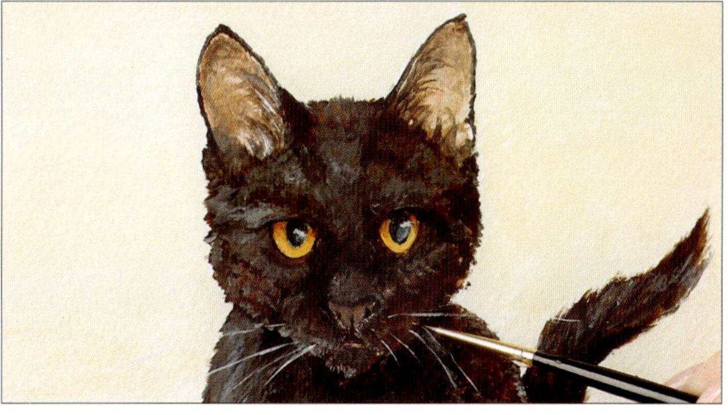

32 Paint in all the details such as the inner ears, eyes, nose and mouth in the same way as for the left-hand cat. Paint in the whiskers on both cats using a size 1 round brush and a mixture of the grey-beige mix and white. For the highlights in the eyes use diluted white and a size 1 round brush.

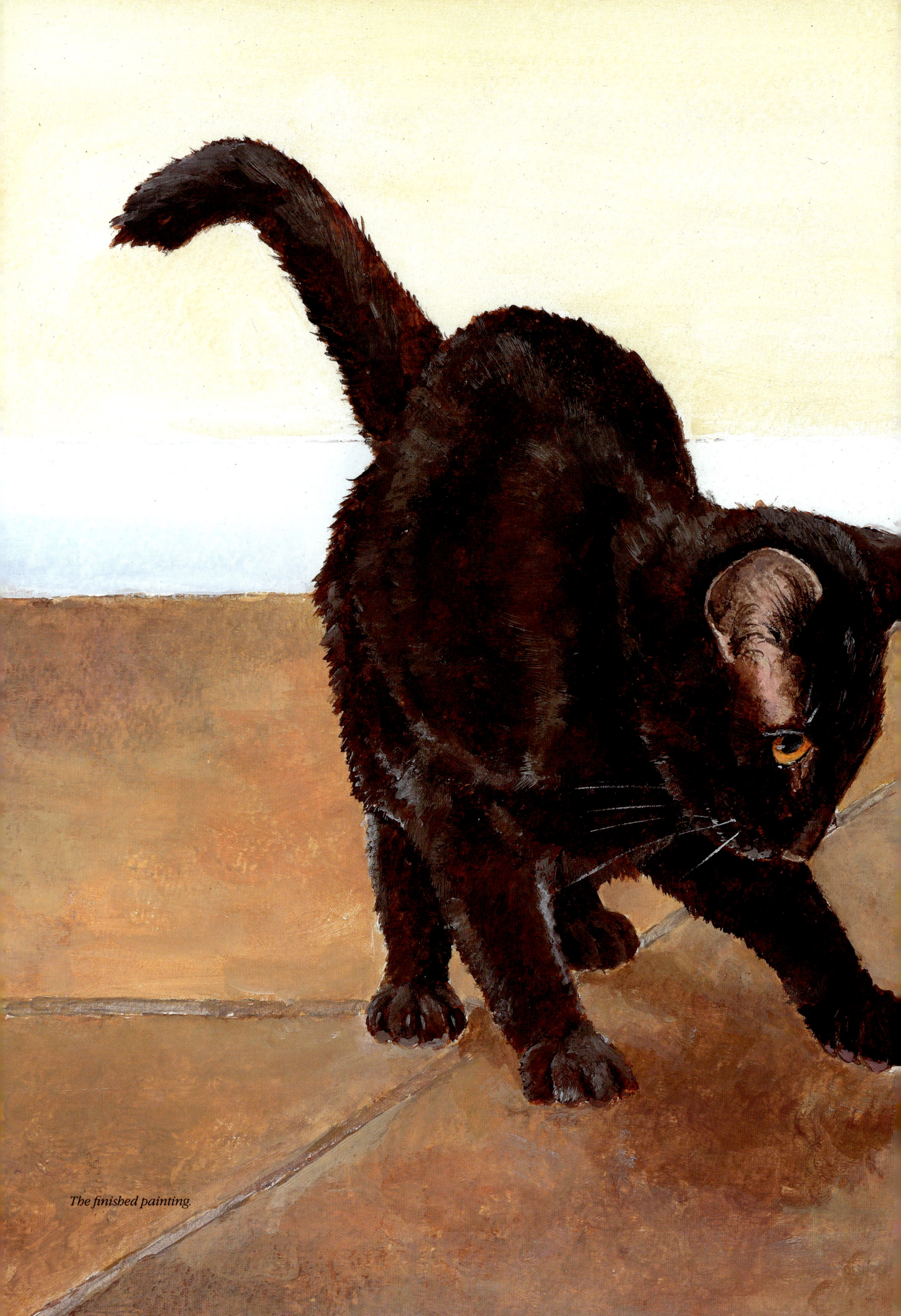

The finished painting.

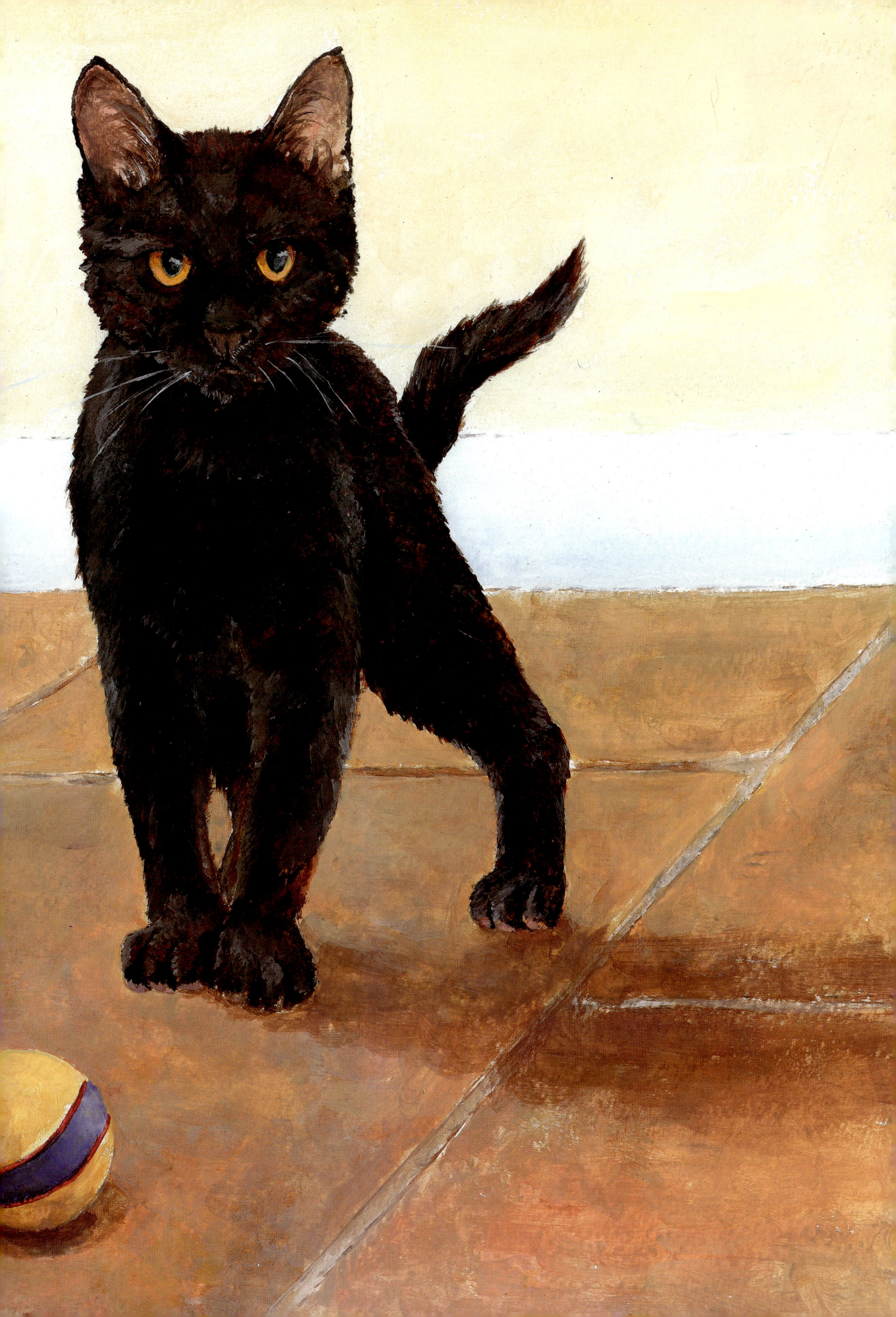

Light Refreshment

A little light refreshment is a must with all that long fur to groom. This cat is a regular visitor to my garden. He knows I always have bowls of water out for my cats and the visiting wildlife. Here he is pausing for a few sips before continuing on his rounds. I think he looks quite serene in the soft light of early morning.

You will need

300gsm (140lb) Rough or Not watercolour paper

Colours: raw sienna, cadmium red, cadmium yellow, cobalt blue, titanium white, cerulean blue, Hooker's green, French ultramarine, burnt umber, yellow ochre, cobalt blue, deep violet

Brushes: size 1 round, size 2 round, size 3 round, 3mm (⅛in) flat, 6mm (¼in), 10mm (⅜in) flat, 15mm (⅝in) flat

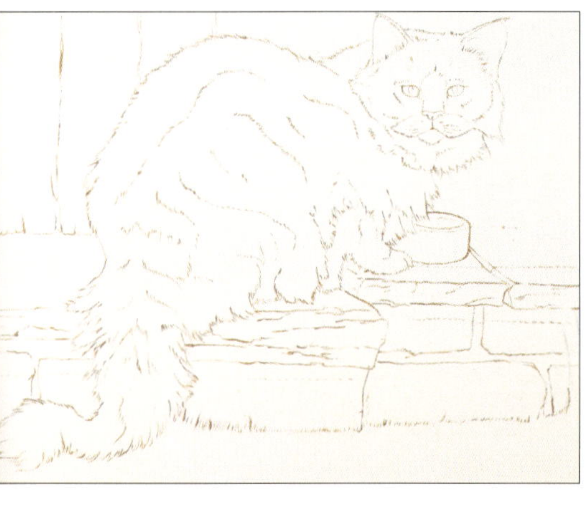

1 Transfer project 5 on to watercolour paper as shown on page 9. Outline the drawing with diluted raw sienna, using a size 1 or 3 round brush.

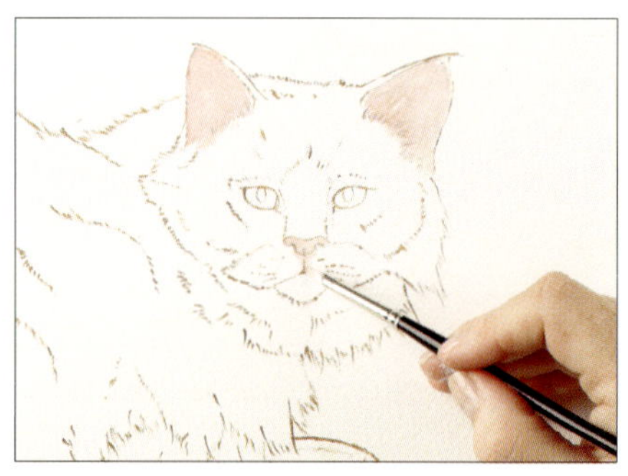

2 Using a 3mm (⅛in) flat brush prepare a pink-lilac mix of mostly white with touches of cadmium red, cadmium yellow and cobalt blue. Block in the nose, inner ears, lips and corners of the eyes.

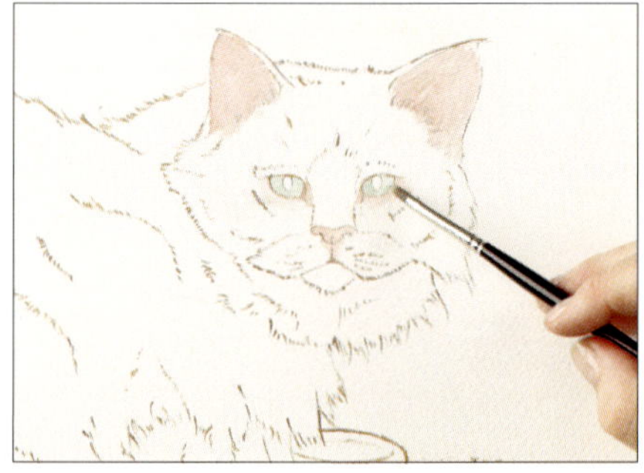

3 Block in the eyes with a mix of cerulean blue, white and cadmium yellow.

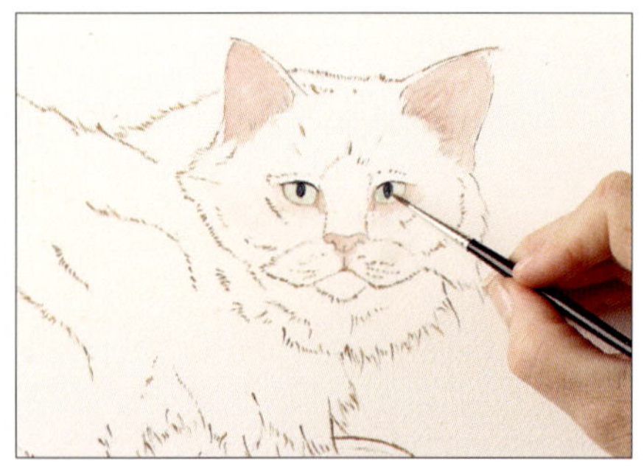

4 Change to a size 2 round brush and using a mix of Hooker's green and French ultramarine, add depth to the pupils. Draw a little of the colour along each eyelid edge.

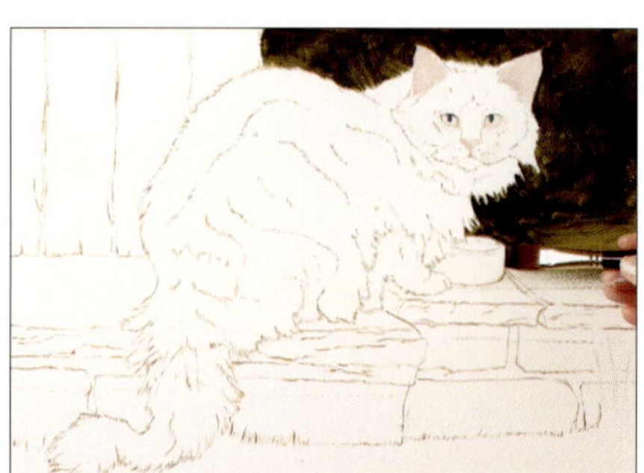

5 Change to a 15mm (⅝in) flat and prepare a dark green background mix of Hooker's green and burnt umber. Block in the right side of the background where the foliage is and feather down towards the wall. Swap to a size 2 round brush to work on the more fiddly areas.

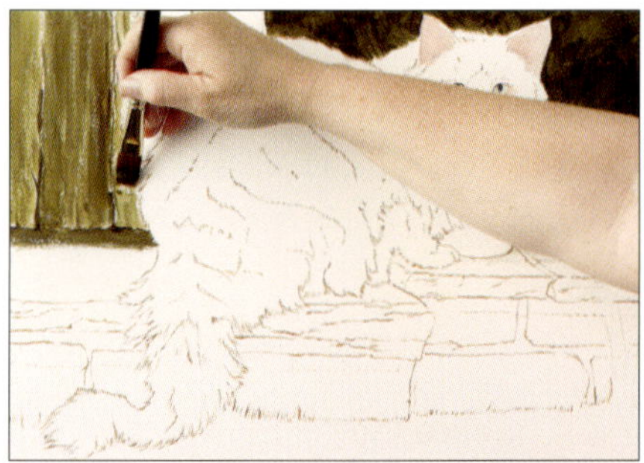

6 Add some yellow ochre to the dark green mix to make a dark yellow-green and brush this colour in downward strokes to mark the fence on the left. Repeat with the dark green mix, quite dry, to describe the grain of the wood on the fence panels.

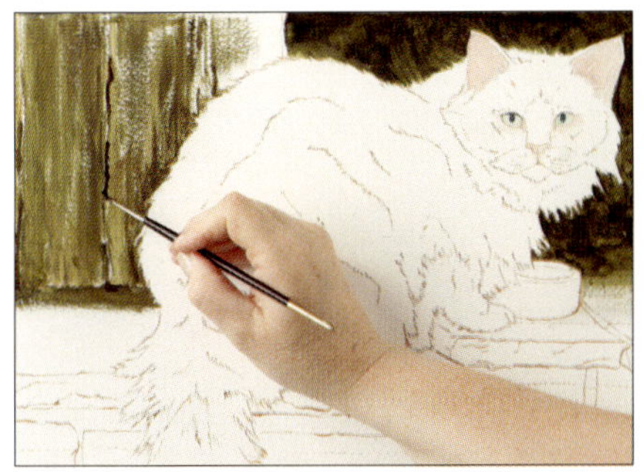

7 Prepare two creamy caramel mixes: white and yellow ochre for a light mix, and white, cadmium red, French ultramarine and yellow ochre for a dark mix. Streak these colours randomly down the fence panels to add age to them. Darken the gaps between the fence panels using the dark green mix (step 5), applied quite patchily.

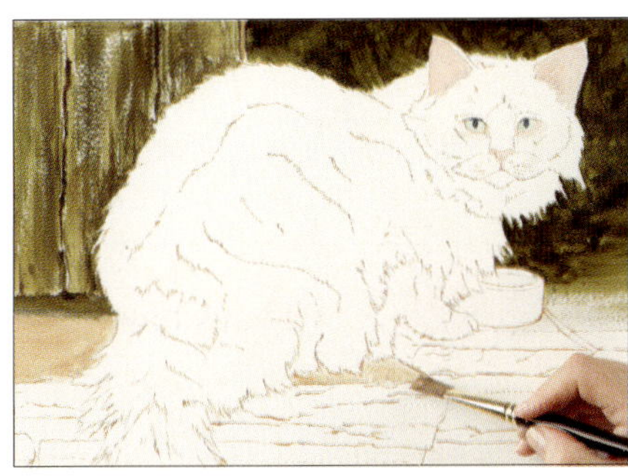

8 Use the dark caramel mix to block in some base tone on the ground.

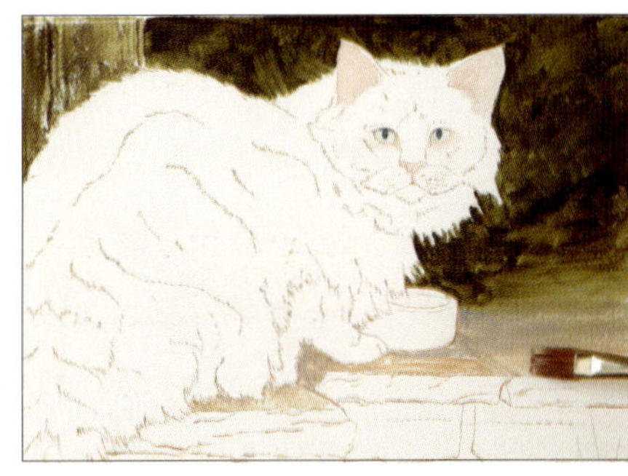

9 Add touches of cobalt blue for shadow – when applied to the caramel base colour it will produce a grey shade.

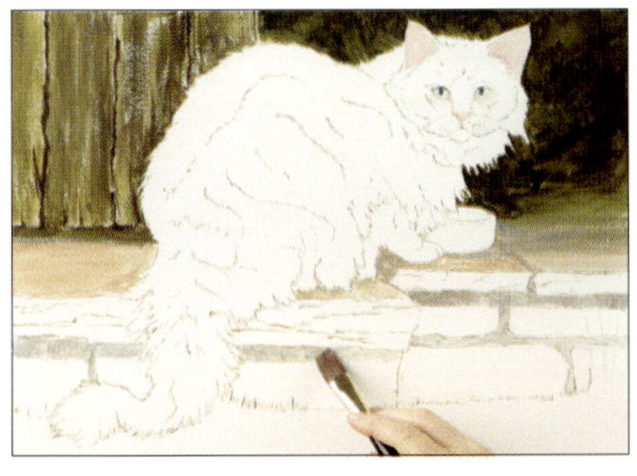

10 Apply the same grey colour to the recesses between the stone wall slabs.

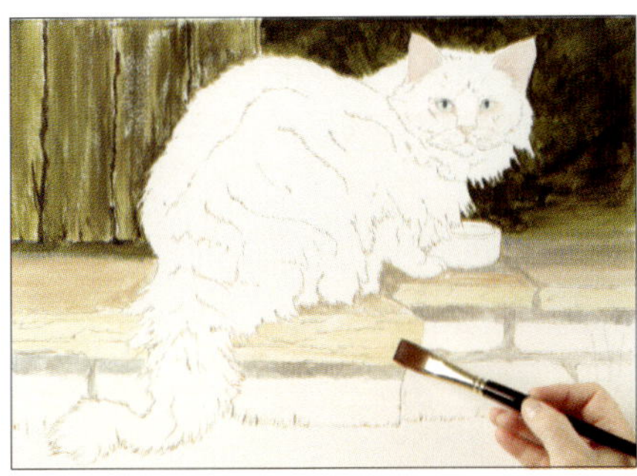

11 Mix yellow ochre, dark caramel and white and block in the top stone slabs. Use a smaller brush round the cat if you find this easier.

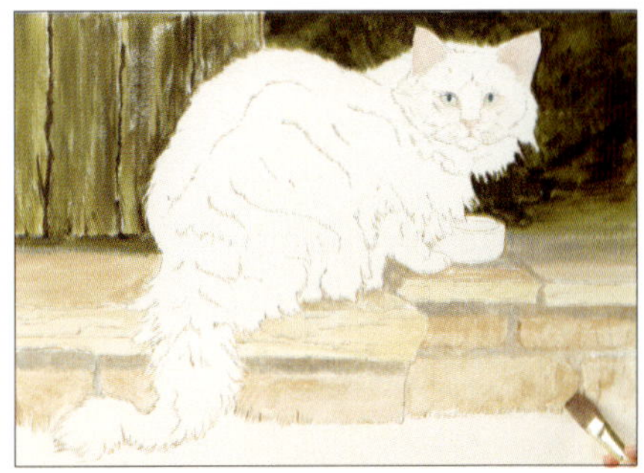

12 Return to the caramel base mix and block in the remaining stone slabs. Take this colour over the grey recesses too.

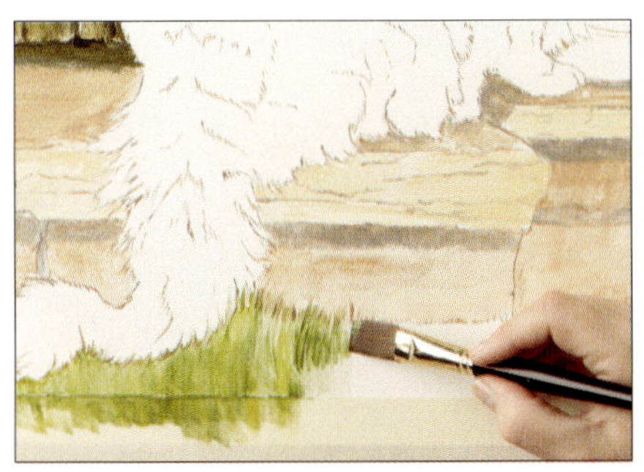

13 Prepare three shades of green: cerulean blue, cadmium yellow and white for a pale green, cerulean blue with more yellow to make a yellow-green and equal parts of cadmium yellow and cerulean blue for a mid-green. Start with the mid-green and, using a 15mm (⅝in) flat brush, block in the grass area. Paint around the tail fur and pull the paint down.

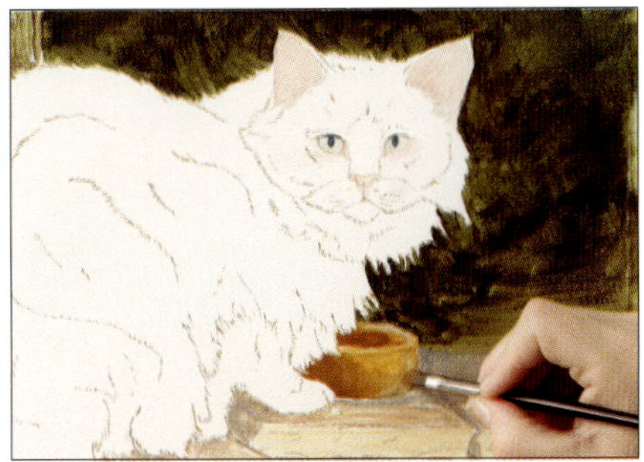

14 Change to a 6mm (¼in) flat brush and using the dark caramel mix, block in the cat's bowl. Use the light caramel mix for the lighter areas and the dark caramel for the shadowed areas. Add a speck of deep violet to darken the caramel mix.

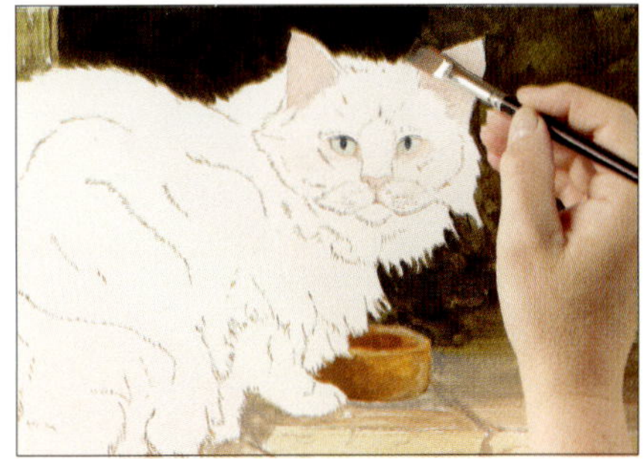

15 Change to a 10mm (⅜in) flat brush and go back over the right side of the background with the dark green foliage colour, to darken it. Work your brush in the opposite direction to how you applied the paint originally to produce texture.

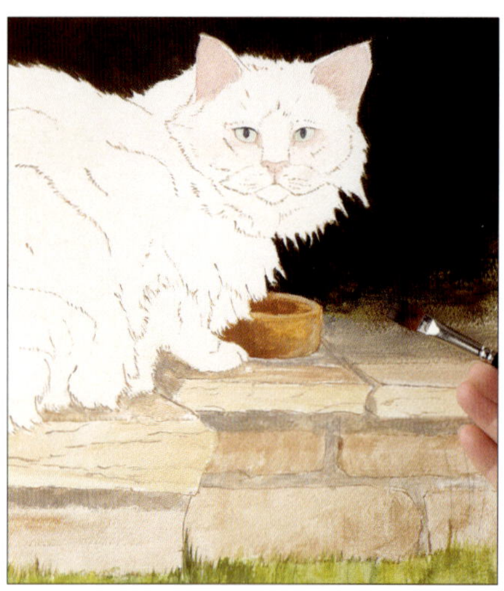

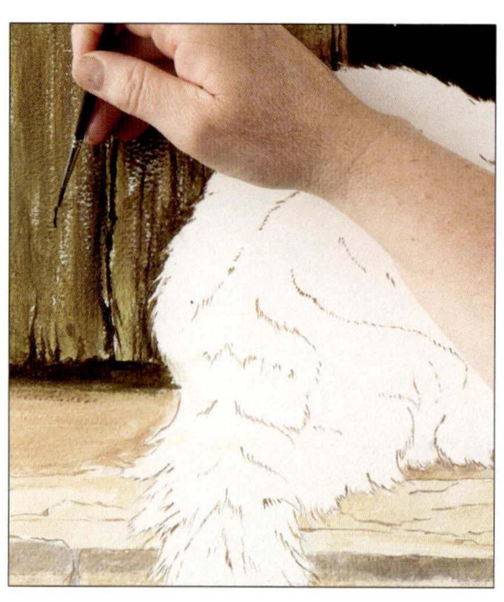

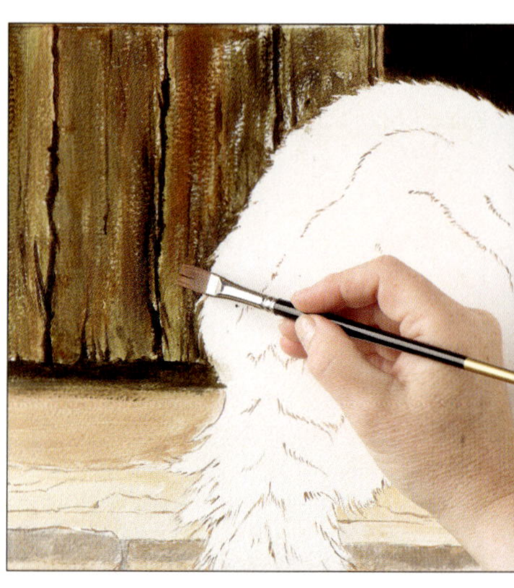

16 Dry brush the dark green area at the bottom right edge of the background foliage.

17 Add some dark green to the bottom of the fence and to the cracks and work it up using your original fence colours. Allow to dry.

18 Glaze over the fence with the dark caramel colour. Alternate between flat strokes and using the side of the brush to add streakiness to the fence, to describe the grain of the wood.

Tip

If you feel your paint is too thick, you can lift some off by dragging kitchen paper down the fence panels.

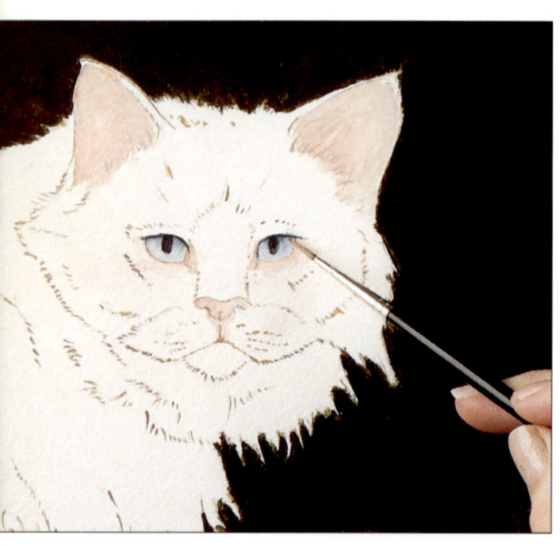

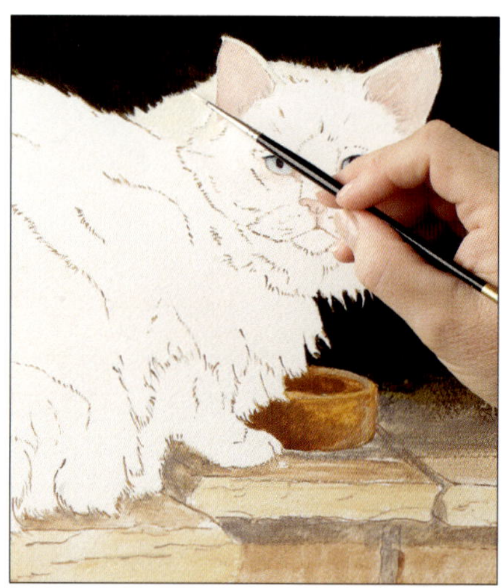

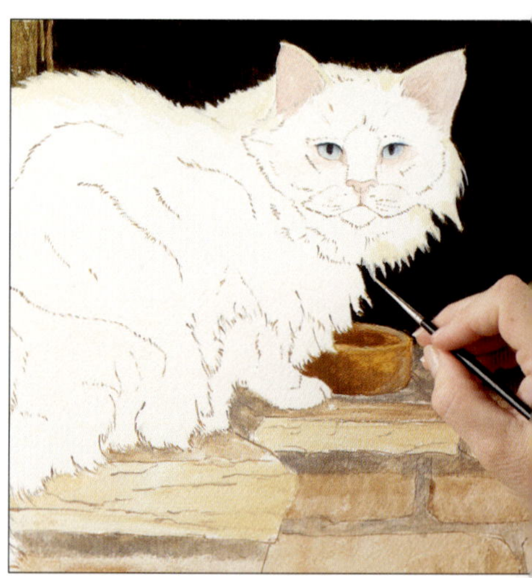

19 Rework the eyes using a size 1 round brush to strengthen the colour and run a line under each eyelid. Apply the cerulean blue to the irises, darker at the top and lighter at the bottom.

20 Apply some of the light caramel mix to the cat's fur; start at the edges and block in a section at a time.

21 Define the strands of hair from the cat's fur where it touches the background.

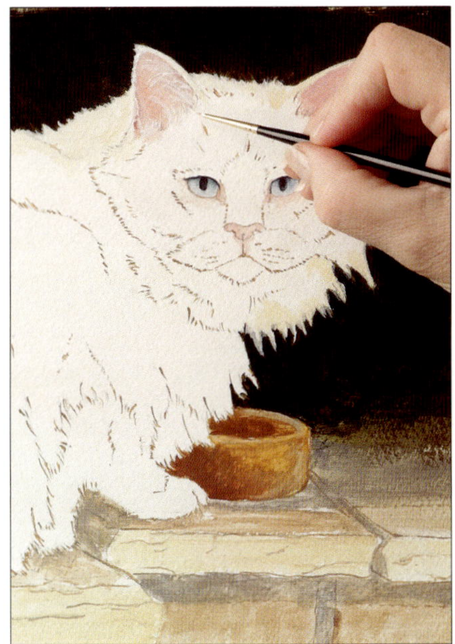

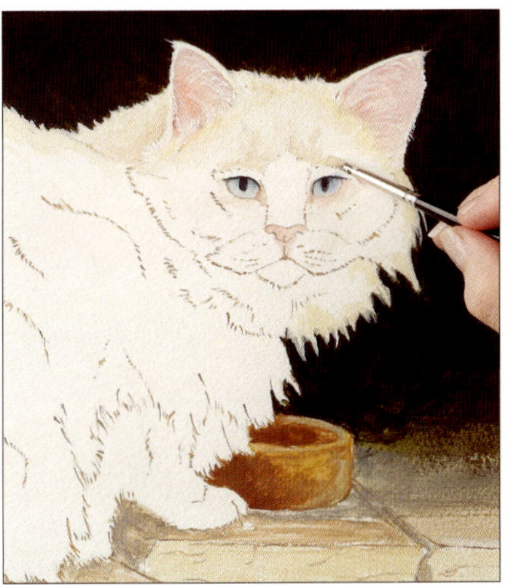

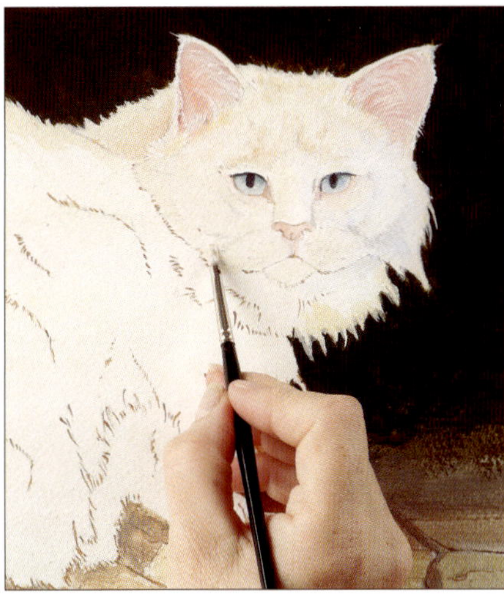

22 Add some pink-lilac and grey tones (using the mix from step 9) into the inner ears for shadow. Change to a size 3 round brush and apply pure white to the sides of the ear to define them, pulling out some tufts of hair to describe the cat's fluffiness.

23 Using the light caramel colour and pure white, start to paint in the cat's face. Start with the pale caramel tones and slowly add white and lighter tones to build up depth.

24 Add touches of cerulean blue to the white on the face to vary the shadows and tones.

Tip

To give depth to pale fur, use pale creams and blues for the under layer and lighter shades for the top fur.

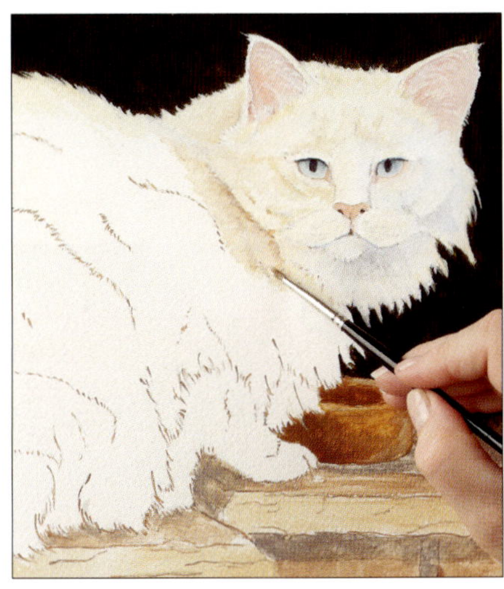

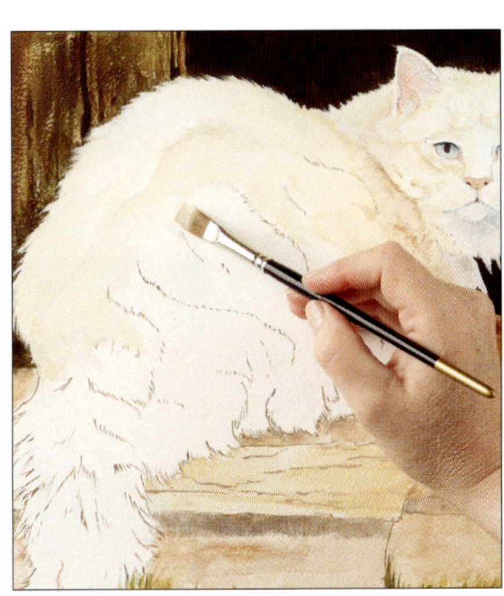

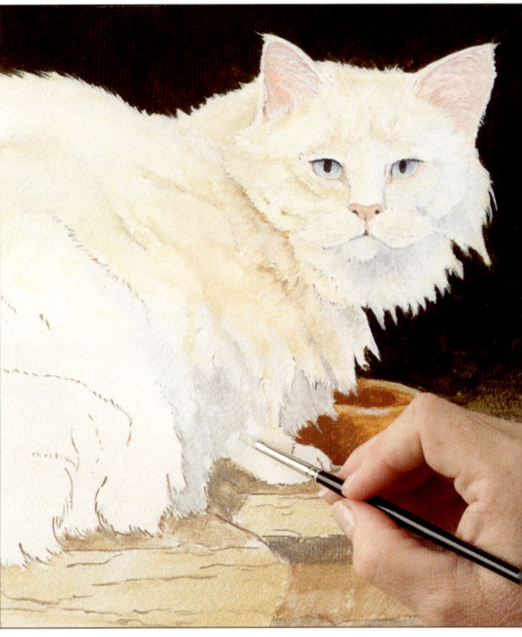

25 Add pale grey shades using various mixes of white, caramel and cerulean blue, and blend into the caramel, cream and white tones.

26 Change to a 10mm (⅜in) flat brush for blocking in the light, creamy caramel colour on the cat.

27 Change to a 3mm (⅛in) flat brush to define the shadowed areas on the cat's fur.

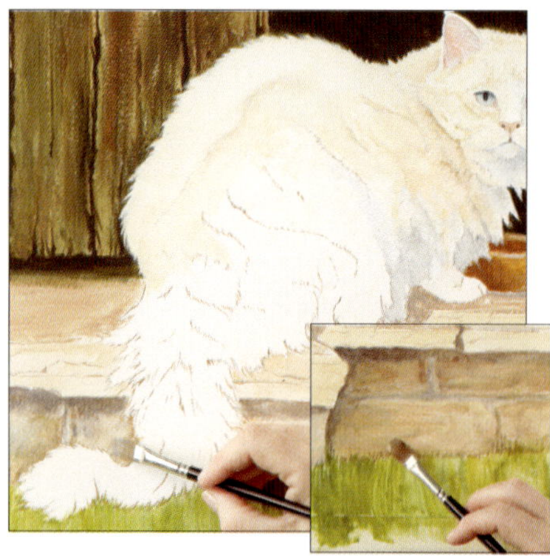 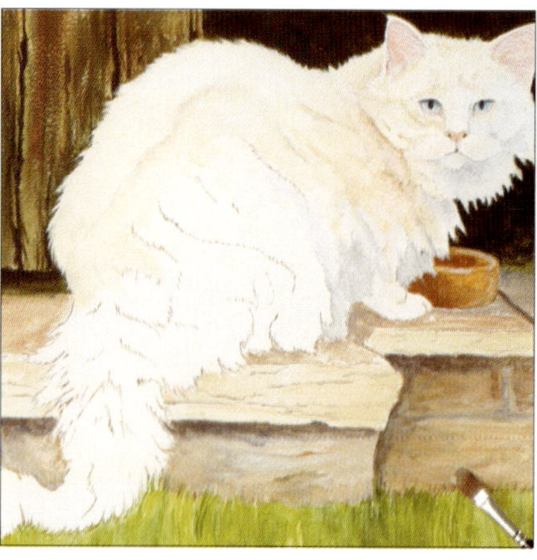 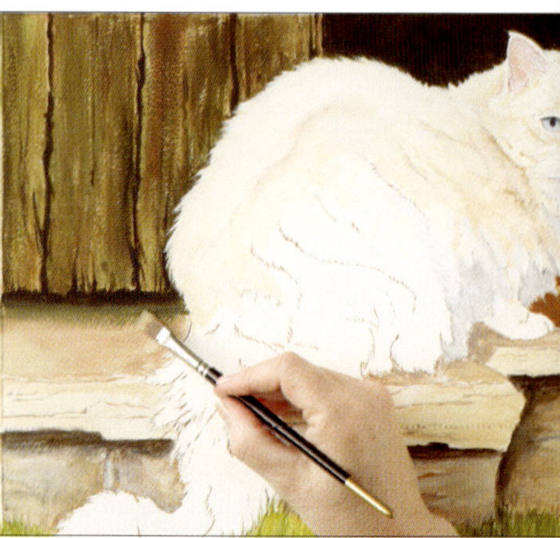

28 For the stone slab wall, change back to a 10mm (⅜in) flat brush and return to the colours you used for the stone slabs. Use a size 2 round brush to paint in the more fiddly areas such as the cat's tail. Mottle the colours to achieve more texture and layer the various shades over each other. Work from left to right across the stone slab wall.

29 Add more shadow to the paving slabs which are directly underneath where the cat is sitting.

30 Prepare a sage green by mixing Hooker's green and the light caramel mix. Use this shade to paint moss on to the base of the fence panels.

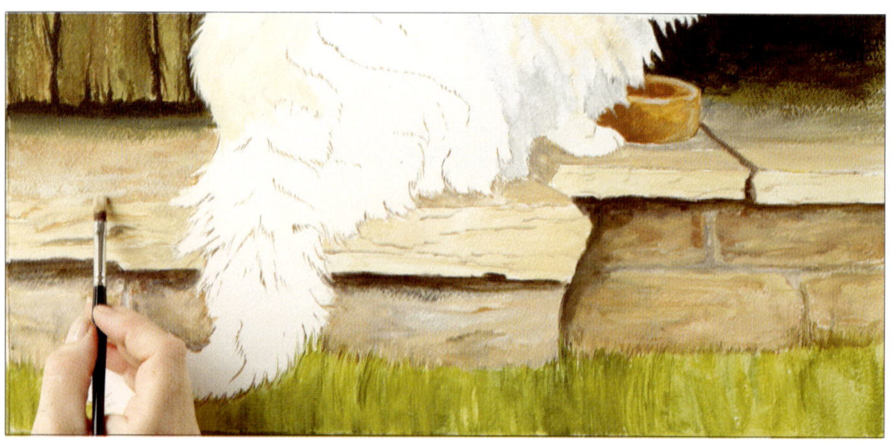

31 Build up the paving slabs using the original caramel and grey colour mixes, layering and scumbling over the base colours. Use a mixture of flat and brush-edge strokes.

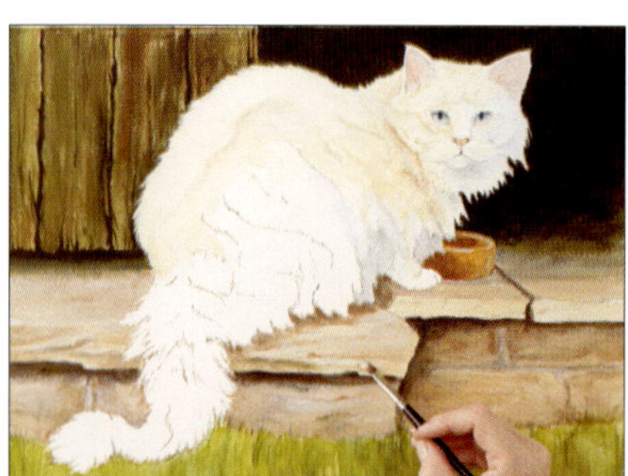 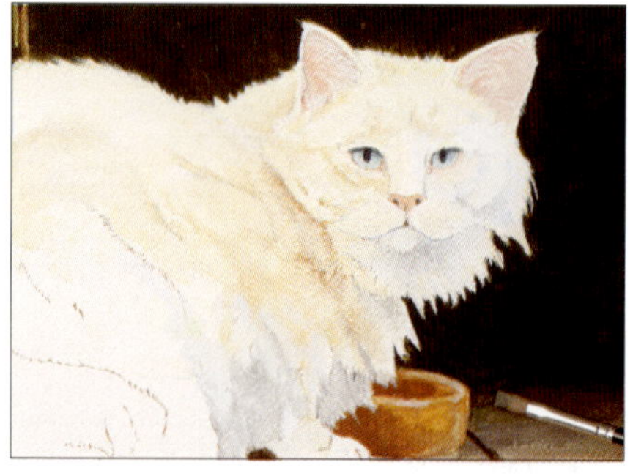 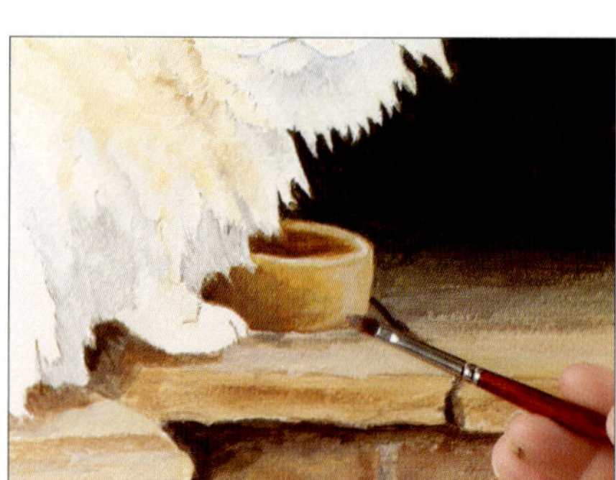

32 Darken the shadows underneath the cat using the dark caramel shade and define the edges of the stone slabs.

33 Go back over the bottom right section of the background with a mix of Hooker's green and French ultramarine and blend with some grey for shadows.

34 Redefine the edges of the cat's bowl using the light and dark caramel colours to sharpen and neaten it up.

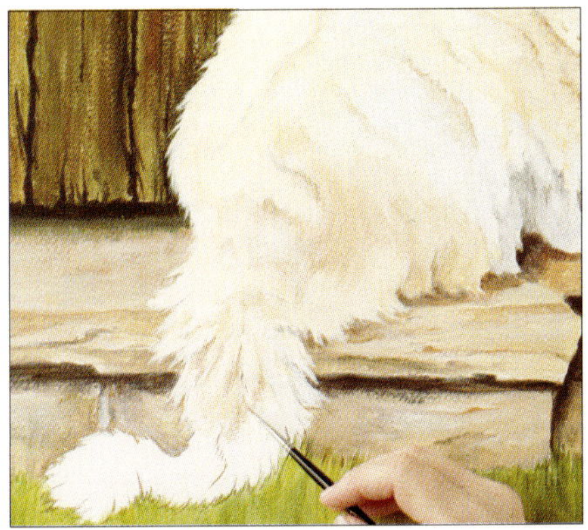

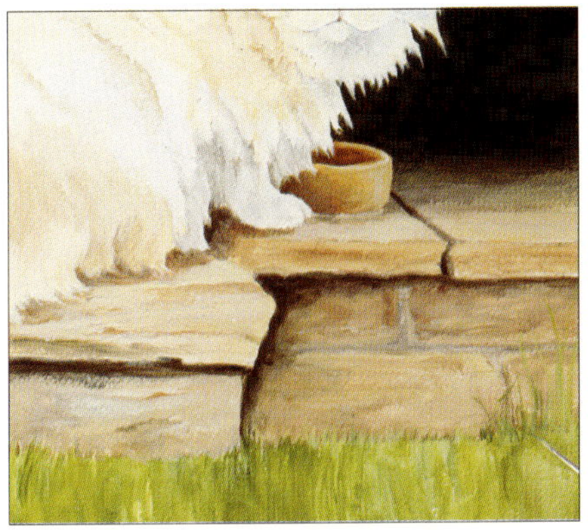

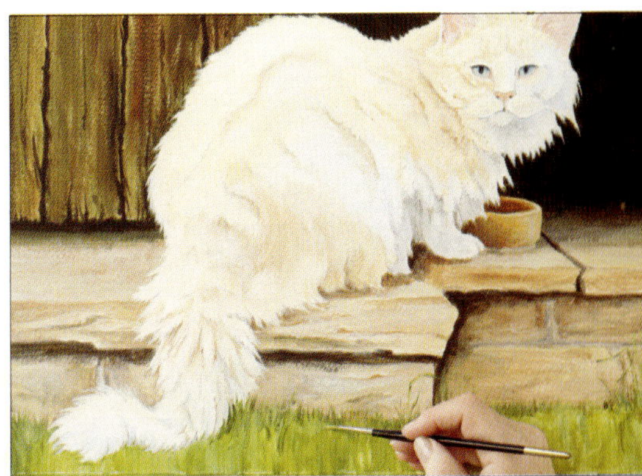

35 Return to working on the cat's fur and work your way down the tail using the same technique as used to work up the fur in the previous steps.

36 Change to a size 2 round brush and using the pale green shade (step 13) and a fairly free stroke, work up the blades of grass against the stone wall.

37 Work in the blades of grass in your varying green shades to create texture and movement and a more realistic finish. Mix some yellow ochre into some of the green shades in places.

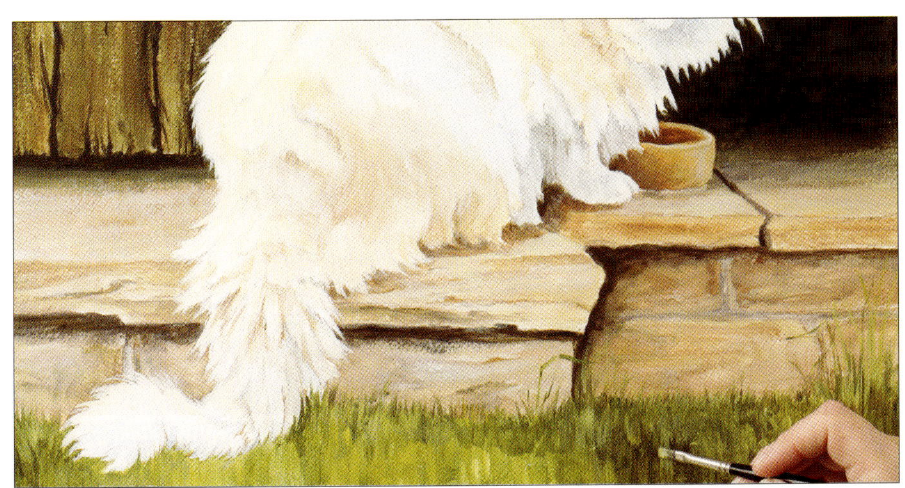

38 For the darker areas of the grass, use the dark green foliage colour (step 5). Continue painting in the grass in these varying shades across the lawn area.

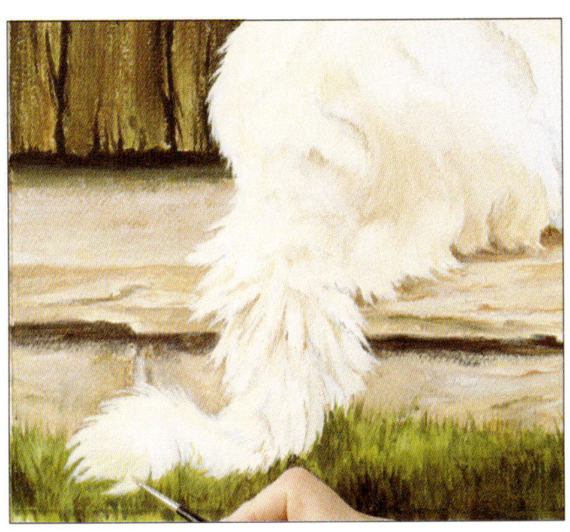

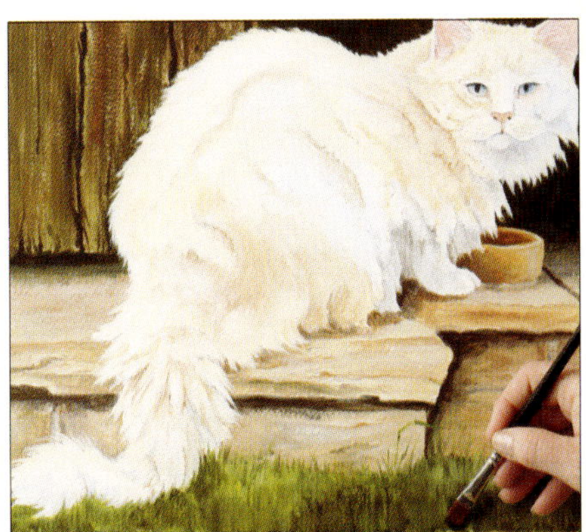

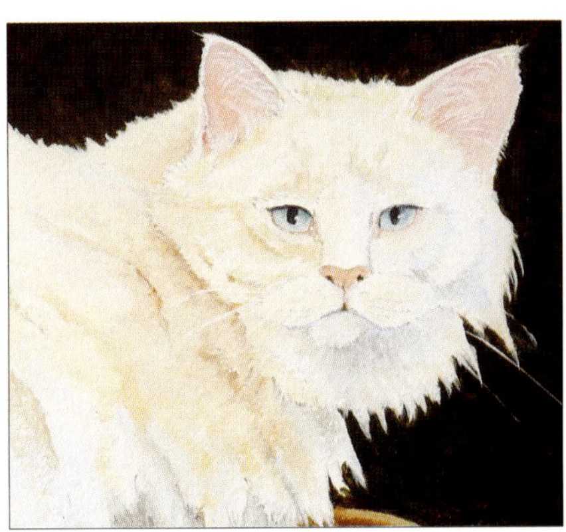

39 Using a size 2 round brush, add brushstrokes of pale green on the cat's tail to show where the blades of grass and the fur meet.

40 Apply a final thin glaze of pale green across the grass with the 10mm (⅜in) flat brush. This will pull all the grass colours together in a unified way.

41 Using a size 3 round brush, loaded with white paint and slightly thinned with water, add in the white highlights on the eyes and the whiskers.

Overleaf

The finished painting.

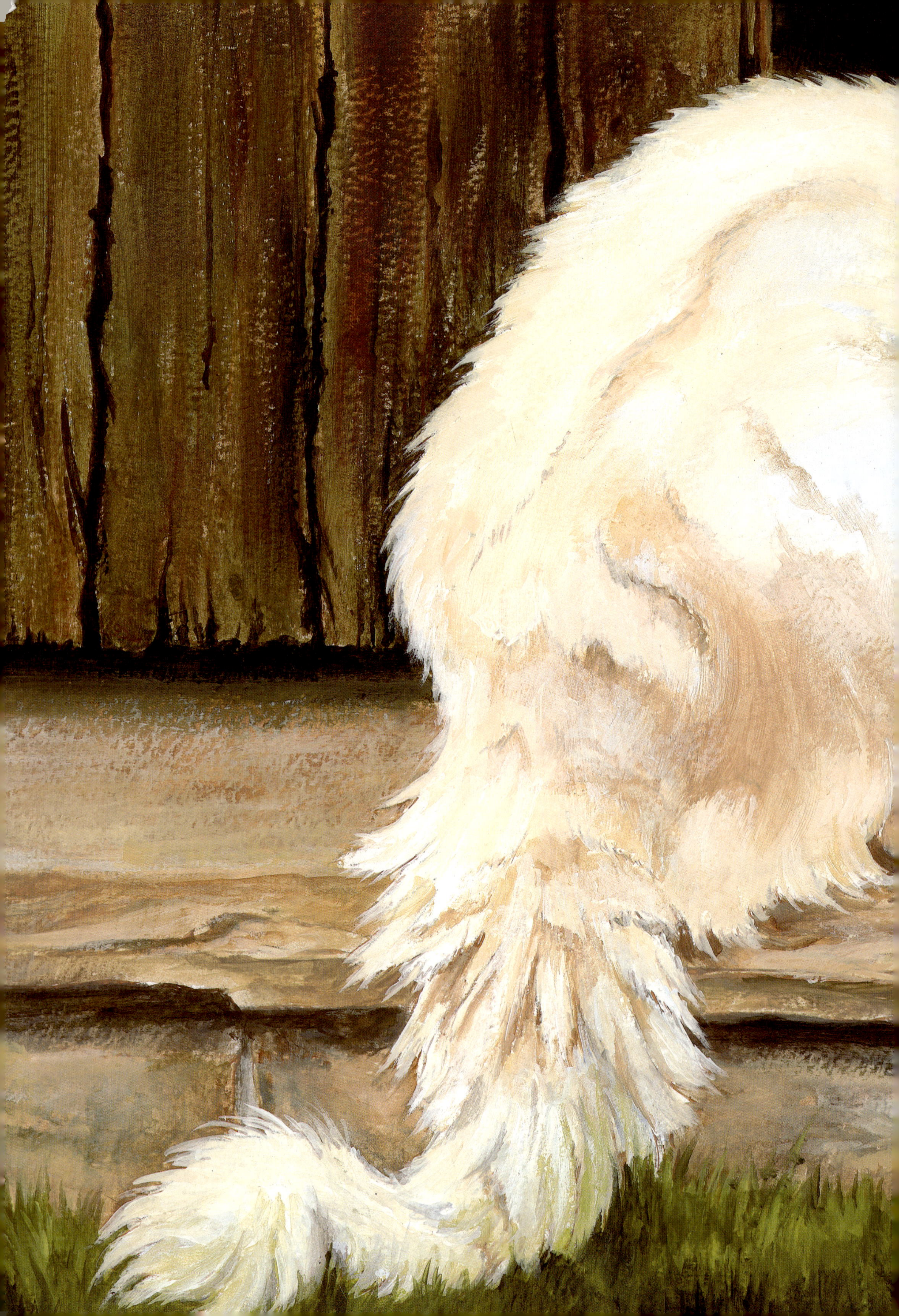

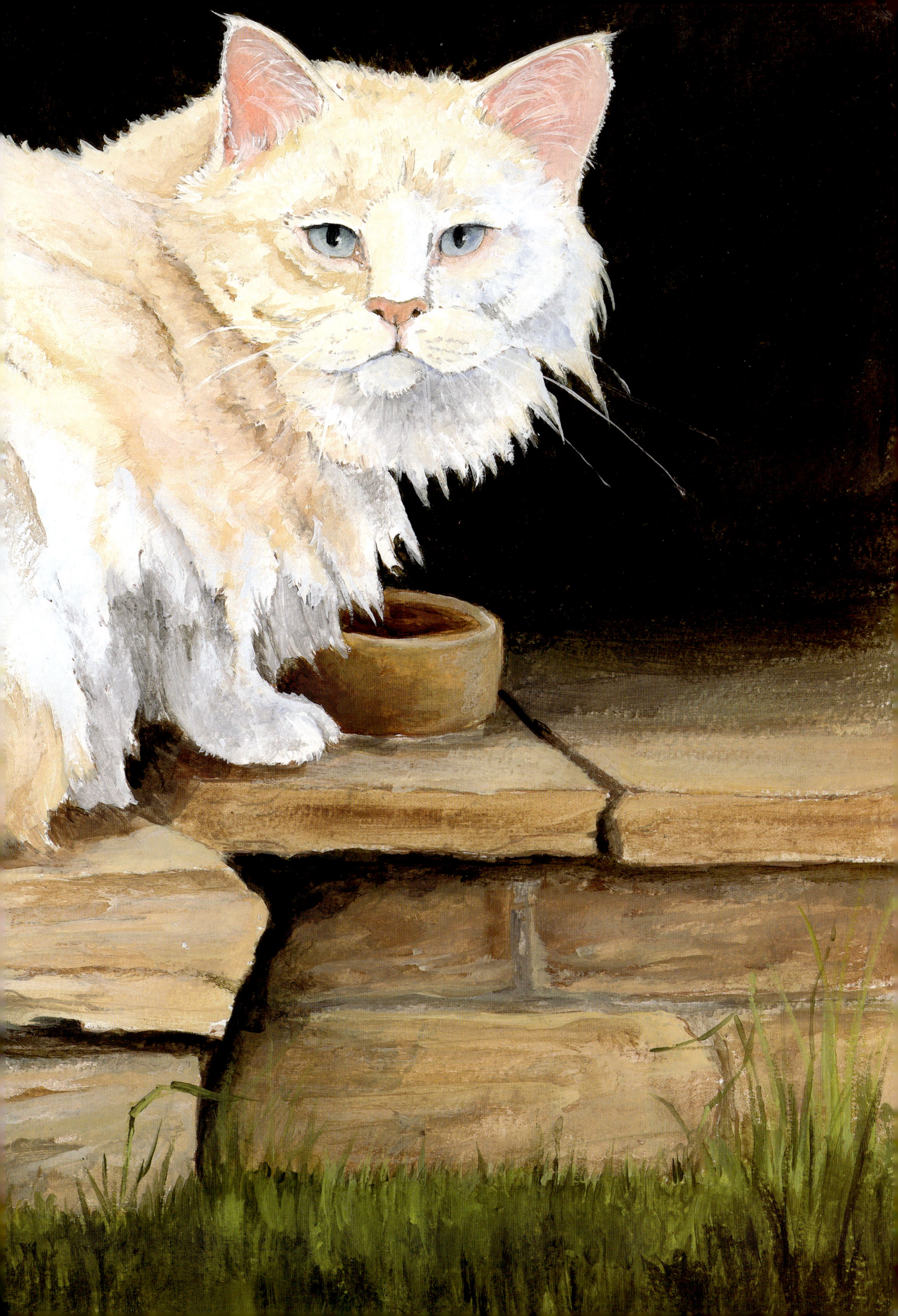

Index

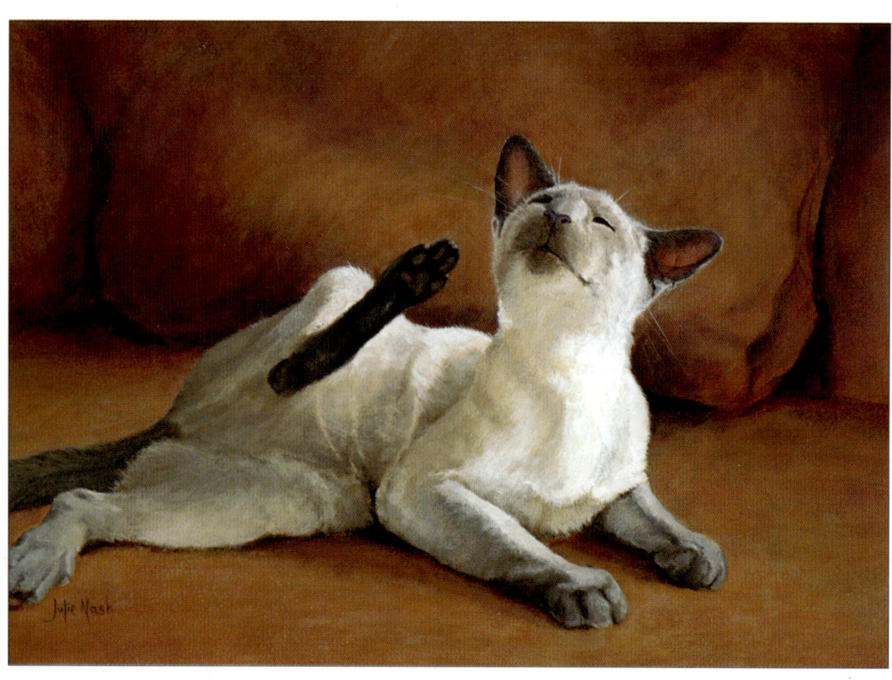

Itchy Chin

42 x 30cm (16½ x 11¾in)

I liked this unusual viewpoint. It's a familiar one for cat owners, but I haven't seen it painted before. I wanted to show the suppleness of the animal and the subtle shades of its silky fur.